# Which? Way to Clean It

## About the author

Cassandra Kent is a freelance journalist, author and broadcaster specialising in consumer affairs and home management.

She worked for *Which?* magazine, a broadcasting trade union and the Family Planning Association before joining the Good Housekeeping Institute, where she became Director of Research and Testing and Associate Editor (Consumer Affairs) of the magazine. She has served on several consumer committees and is the author of over 20 practical household books. With experience of managing a family and two homes she is an expert on cleaning problems of all kinds, believing there are few that cannot be tackled successfully.

# Which? Way to Clean It

*Cassandra Kent*

 CONSUMERS' ASSOCIATION

Which? Books are commissioned and researched by
Consumers' Association and published by
Which? Ltd, 2 Marylebone Road, London NW1 4DF
Email address: books@which.net

Distributed by The Penguin Group:
Penguin Books Ltd, 80 Strand, London WC2R 0RL

First edition September 1994
Reprinted March 1995, October 1995, June 1996, September 1997
Second edition April 1998
Revised reprint 2001
Third edition 2002

*British Library Cataloguing-in-Publication Data*
A catalogue record for this book is available from the British Library

ISBN 0 85202 871 7

For a full list of Which? books, please write to Which? Books, Castlemead,
Gascoyne Way, Hertford X, SG14 1LH or access our website at *www.which.net*

Acknowledgements: The information on product labelling in Appendix I was supplied by
*Health Which?*

Editorial and production: Alethea Doran, Robert Gray

Cover and text design by Kysen Creative Consultants

Typeset by Saxon Graphics Ltd, Derby
Printed and bound in Great Britain by Clays Ltd, Bungay, Suffolk

# Contents

# Introduction

Some people love cleaning; others detest the task. Whether you like it or loathe it, basic cleaning is essential to maintain hygiene and avoid dirt-induced infections and conditions such as asthma, which can be triggered by house dust. It is work to be achieved as quickly and easily as possible, and, fortunately, is no longer the chore it was when hands, knees and elbow grease played a large part. These days electrical equipment and tools make light work of formerly laborious tasks.

However much or little you choose to do, this book will help you work efficiently. It explains how to establish a manageable routine, tells you which products are the most effective for specific items or materials, and suggests when you would be wise to entrust a cleaning problem to an expert. It takes the mystery out of cleaning and tells you – at least as important as *what* to do – what *not* to do.

## Keeping on top of it all

It is hard to maintain order, let alone cleanliness, if you are running a busy home. Persuading children, especially teenagers, to clean up after themselves is a thankless task, but you can encourage everyone to do their bit to help things run smoothly. Even if your home is not spotless, it will look cleaner if it is kept tidy, with the detritus of everyday living in its place or out of sight. This does not mean, of course, stuffing dirty socks down the sofa, but remembering to put them in the laundry bin. Encourage small children to put toys away in large plastic bins each evening rather than leaving them as hazards strewn around the house to be tripped over. Ask teenagers to keep their personal clutter in their bedrooms – where you can ignore it.

If you cannot face cleaning up in the evening, have a quick blitz in the morning to get rid of débris such as cigarette stubs or crisp packets.

If you are in a hurry, put dirty cups, plates, etc. into a bowl of water and washing-up liquid to await your return from work or the school run.

## Laundering

Laundry is one of the major cleaning tasks in the home, since clothes, as well as bodies, need to be cleaned frequently. Again, if you have a family you will need to resign yourself to spending a fair amount of time on laundry, as babies and children get dirty rapidly. Clothes will get smellier if you smoke, use public transport or eat a lot of highly flavoured food such as curries. Ignore the myth that living in a town is dirtier than in the country – the latter is just a different kind of dirt: mud as opposed to grime.

Disaster stories about washing clothes and other fabric items abound. Which of us has not been tempted to save money by washing by hand something that screams 'dry-clean only'? While this may be a risk worth taking with cheap clothes, take heed from the mistake of the woman who, appalled by the estimate for dry-cleaning her expensive curtains, decided to hand-wash them in the bath. The result? Shrinkage, colour run, puckering – and a bill for new curtains.

Many of us have had the sorry experience of doing a mixed colour and white wash only to discover that the entire household's underwear is now a mucky pink. (Thank goodness for those products that enable you to get the dye out – but be sure to follow the instructions, which usually involve soaking in a sink, *not* in a washing machine.) Don't mix whites and colours unless you're positive they won't run, and always wash new, deep-dyed items separately until you are sure they have stopped shedding dye. Red dye is a particularly bad culprit.

## Getting help

If you can afford it, reliable cleaning help is a boon beyond belief. Information on hiring help with cleaning is provided in Chapter 1. Bear in mind, of course, that this is a working relationship: you are the employer, not a counsellor to discuss bad backs, medical operations or relationship problems over tea and biscuits. If you're not getting value for money or the kind of help you need, look elsewhere.

Getting friends to help is a good idea only if they are dependable (for example, not prone to dropping things), know where the various objects in your home live, and, most importantly, know how to clean what – especially where valuable items are concerned. There are plenty of horror stories about well-meaning helpers putting the best cut-glass in the dishwasher or scrubbing silver cutlery with a scouring pad. If you have items of either monetary or sentimental value, you may prefer to clean them yourself rather than risk damage to them.

## Using this book

*Which? Way to Clean It* covers cleaning in all areas of the home. The book is divided into parts that deal with particular items, materials and stains; different areas of the home; the garden; and even pets and pests. Each section is dotted with tip boxes giving useful hints to make your cleaning jobs even easier. Use the index and cross-references to find the section you want at a glance.

Chapter 9, Products that work, is a list of cleaning products which do just that. Some are widely available in the shops, others by mail order only. Details of suppliers are provided in the Addresses section, which also includes many useful specialist manufacturers, services and trade organisations, relating to all areas covered in the book.

Over the past decade or so, the most noticeable change in the range of cleaning products on shop shelves is the growing number of those claiming to be 'green'. Appendix I, Chemicals in cleaning products, outlines the issues in this area. It describes the possible implications for both our health and the environment, and tells you how to find out more.

It is well known that a high proportion of accidents happen in the home, in the course of domestic cleaning and repair work. Appendix II, Safety and first aid, explains the safety precautions that should always be observed when engaged in these activities, and details basic first-aid procedures for different types of injuries.

## Successful cleaning

Some final advice: think clean, but do not become a slave to cleanliness. Your time and effort are valuable commodities, so take advantage of every labour-saving trick and worthwhile product you can. We hope that *Which? Way to Clean It* will enable you to achieve great results in as much – or as little – time as you wish to spend.

Chapter 1

# Organising your cleaning

Keeping your home clean need not be an endless, time-consuming, back-breaking chore; gone are the days of black-leading grates, brushing stairs on hands and knees and beating rugs with wooden sticks. Nowadays, there is a product or appliance to clean almost anything in your home, and although manufacturers would like you to believe that all their cleaning products are essential, all you really need are some key items.

Bulk buying can save money, but people tend to use more than necessary with large-sized products, so theoretical savings can get swallowed up. If you have access to bulk sources, decant suitable quantities into standard-sized containers and refill when necessary.

Be sure to label the new containers clearly and indelibly. Stick-on labels, which may fall off, are not satisfactory – particularly where poisonous chemicals are concerned.

In general, paying more for standard-sized cleaning products means you get stronger, better-quality goods. But if your household is profligate with cleaning products it may be more economical to buy cheaper, less concentrated brands and shop more frequently for replacements. Even if a product claims to be 'concentrated', most people tend to employ the amount they usually use, regardless of the quantity recommended on the container.

This book will tell you what products to use, how to clean things as easily as possible and how to organise your cleaning to save yourself time and energy. Work out a routine that suits you and stick to it. Do not panic if you sometimes skip cleaning; dust is only a worry if you or someone in your family suffers from asthma or an allergy to house dust. Most importantly for health, keep kitchens and lavatories clean.

## Setting up a cleaning file

A cleaning file can save hours of frustration, especially for those items which rarely need cleaning, but which need to be cleaned in a particular way using specialist products. Put laundering and cleaning instructions for all your upholstery, furniture, surfaces, household items and clothes in a ring binder so that you can refer to them quickly. Keep a note of any successful stain removal or cleaning treatments. You do not need to be very organised about the file as long as you put the instructions into it when you buy something new and label them with what they refer to.

If you are moving into a new home where the cooker and carpets are being left, try to get care information from the departing owners before they leave – and file it. Most of the time you will not need to refer to the file but the information will be there should you need it. Make sure that you label any instructions which do not carry a brand name, to make clear what item the label came off.

## Cleaning products

Don't be swayed by labels which state that products are suitable for kitchen-only or bathroom-only cleaning. Most such products work equally well in both areas, so it is pointless to buy both, especially if you are on a tight budget – unless you want to keep the cleaners in separate rooms.

### *Essential products*
The absolute basics for most homes are:

- washing-up liquid
- mild household detergent
- abrasive household detergent
- biological washing powder
- specialist metal cleaners
- furniture polish
- a selection of detergents and soapflakes for laundry.

It is also useful to keep ammonia, white spirit, turpentine, laundry borax, bicarbonate of soda, bleach, methylated spirit, washing soda and white vinegar in stock as they can be used to clean a vast number of household surfaces.

> Bars of soap will last longer if you store them in the airing cupboard.

## Cleaning tools

There is no need to cram your cupboard full of every cleaning gadget in existence. Most household tasks can be tackled with a few items and you should invest in more specialised equipment only if it proves necessary.

11

### Essential equipment

The basic tools for your cleaning routine should be:

- vacuum cleaner
- hard-/soft-bristled brooms
- dustpan and hard-/soft-bristled brushes
- lavatory brush and holder
- cellulose sponges (old loofahs make excellent cleaning pads)
- squeegee floor mop and bucket
- buckets and bowls
- dusters and polishing cloths
- a couple of chamois leathers
- washing-up utensils
- household gloves – keep separate pairs for specific tasks such as washing-up, lavatory-cleaning, etc.
- a nose-and-mouth mask to prevent inhalation of fumes given off by certain cleaning products
- a kneeler, which you may need from time to time to strip off floor polish or clean a floor on your hands and knees.

---

If your fingernails are long, rubber gloves will last longer if you turn them inside out and stick a small piece of waterproof plaster in each fingertip, before turning them the right way out again.

---

### Vacuum cleaner

It is important that you have a vacuum cleaner that is right for you and your home. The table opposite shows the pros and cons of the different types available. The following is a checklist of points you should consider when buying.

- Does it run smoothly?
- Is it the right height for you?
- Are the attachments easy to fit?
- Does it suit your home (i.e. the amount of space, stairs and types of surfaces)?
- If you suffer from allergies or asthma, is the vacuum cleaner designed to eliminate more dust than standard models?
- Does it have a retractable cable or other means of storing the cable neatly?

| Type of vacuum cleaner | Good points | Bad points |
|---|---|---|
| Upright | Good beating action. Covers large areas fast. Suction can be set to clean hard floors. | Not good at getting into corners or under low furniture. Not convenient for stairs. Not suitable for loop-pile carpets. |
| Cylinder | Flexible hose ideal for stairs and for getting under furniture. Good for cleaning upholstery and curtains. | Flexible hose can kink. Trailing the cleaner behind you can be cumbersome. |
| Multipurpose | Cleans carpets and hard floors. Can be used to shampoo carpets, and can vacuum up water. | Bulky to store. Expensive. Can be noisy. |
| Hand-held cordless | Good for cars, carpet edges, cupboards and picking up crumbs. | Needs recharging after a few minutes of vacuuming. No good for large surfaces. |
| Miniature | Suitable for cars, hobby work and home office equipment. | Not designed for domestic use, very small capacity. |
| Built-in system (Hose plugs into outlet; dust collected goes into central bin.) | You do not have to carry the cleaner around with you – useful if you find lifting difficult. The bin should not need to be emptied often | Unless the system is installed when the house or flat is built, dust pipes running down walls may be visible. |

Making maximum use of vacuum cleaner **attachments** will eliminate the need for a lot of manual dusting. You can use them to clean walls, curtains, upholstery, glazed pictures, mirrors and so on.

The crevice tool can reach awkward areas and clean right up to the skirting boards.

The upholstery tool is for soft surfaces, curtains, mattresses and some stairs.

The soft round dusting brush is for cleaning picture rails, dado rails, banisters and carved wood.

## Cleaning routines

Following a simple routine is the most effective way of maintaining cleanliness. Divide your home and its contents into three or four categories: things that need daily cleaning (surfaces and items used most frequently), things that need regular cleaning, things that need occasional cleaning and things which require a once-yearly blitz.

You will save yourself time and effort by maintaining a routine and not allowing things to get so dirty that cleaning them is a huge and tedious job. Save major cleaning for when you have time to complete it.

Recruit a family member or friend to help; it will take far less time if you work together. For example, if your helper empties cupboards and washes the contents, you can be cleaning the cupboards themselves and putting things back.

Wear sensible or old clothes for cleaning, preferably made from natural fibres which are more comfortable and less sweaty. Protect hands with rubber or cotton gloves or use a barrier cream.

### Daily cleaning

Lavatories and kitchen surfaces should be cleaned daily. Try to wash up, tidy the kitchen and wipe over all the work surfaces once a day with a cleaner that contains a bactericide – this should keep germs at bay. If you have pets that walk on worktops (this should not be encouraged) you should always prepare food on chopping boards that are stored away from where they walk.

It takes at least half an hour for the moisture lost by bodies overnight to evaporate, so air and make beds before you go out in the morning. Ideally, you should throw back the covers when you get up and make the bed after breakfast. Try to make sure everyone in your home does the same – it makes bedrooms look tidier, cleaner and more welcoming when you get home.

## Regular cleaning

Start by ventilating the room you are going to clean. Closed windows provide insulation and keep out intruders but they also allow smells to build up, and household pests love to breed in the hot humid atmosphere produced by central heating. Research has shown that there are far more allergens in most homes than are found outside.

Next, tidy the room. Throw out dead flowers, clean ashtrays, remove dirty cups and put things back in their right place. If this is all you have time to do, the room will at least *look* cleaner.

When the room is ventilated close the windows before you start cleaning. Sweep or vacuum first as this tends to raise dust. Then dust surfaces and ornaments, applying polish or another cleaning product if needed. Start dusting on one side of a door and work round the room until you reach the other side; in this way no section will be missed. If you are interrupted by the doorbell or a telephone call put your dusters down where you are and you will know where to start again. Always dust higher surfaces first as some dust will fall on to lower ones.

---

### Washing floors

Use two buckets when you wash a floor. Fill one with the cleaning solution, the other with clear warm water. Wet your squeegee mop in the cleaning solution and wash a section of the floor. Rinse the mop in the clean water before putting it back in the cleaning solution. In this way you will not be washing the floor with dirty water. Change the rinsing water as necessary.

---

### Dirt-defying duster

Make a dirt-defying duster by soaking it in an equal mixture of paraffin and vinegar for a couple of hours. Impregnating the duster with oil and acid allows it to pick up dust rather than just spreading it around. Make sure the duster is clean before you start. Store in a lidded container when not in use, wring it out and allow to dry naturally before using, and check that the duster is free of grit before cleaning or polishing anything.

---

### *Special cleaning*

How often a room needs a really good turn-out depends on the general wear and tear to your home. If your regular cleaning routine is reasonably well maintained this will not be very often, but neglecting things for too long results in more work later on.

Use the opportunity of a major turn-out to take down curtains for cleaning, shampoo the carpet and upholstery and clean the walls, windows and so on.

Go through cupboards and drawers and dispose of items that you no longer use.

Mend or take to a professional anything that needs repairing. Take good-quality curtains, rugs and window blinds to reliable professionals if you don't feel able to clean them yourself.

Tackle one room at a time and do not move to another until you have finished the first. Even if you have set aside some days for the task it is almost impossible to maintain the impetus, say, to wash the walls in six rooms. You will feel much more positive if you complete one room at a time.

---

**Broom care**

Wash broom and brush bristles from time to time in a solution of washing-up liquid. Rinse in warm water and then in cold salty water to stiffen the bristles. Hang brooms up by their handles (screw a hook on the end if necessary), as the bristles will be flattened if you stand the broom on them.

---

## Storing cleaners

- Try to keep all your cleaning gear in one place. If your home has several floors you may want to have a cleaning cache on each floor to save carting stuff around – this may be more expensive initially but the cost evens out.
- Do not decant cleaning products into other containers without labelling them clearly and ineradicably.
- Use an old shopping basket or a plastic box to carry your kit around with you while you clean. This saves lots of journeys back and forth.

- Clean your cleaning equipment before you put it away. Check that fluff and hairs are removed from vacuum cleaner attachments, brooms and brushes. Wash dirt and grit out of buckets. Wash or discard dusters and polishing cloths that have become too dirty to re-use.

---

Stitch up the bottom edge of an apron to form a pocket and use it to collect odds and ends found around the house out of their rightful places.

---

## Hiring help with cleaning

Hiring someone else to clean for you only relieves you of the chore if you are cautious about whom you appoint.

Think first about how much help you need. For a small home, three to four hours a week should be enough for routine cleaning plus a few extra non-regular tasks such as polishing silver, cleaning an oven or cleaning windows. A larger home may need more time and if you have a messy household you may prefer to have fewer hours more frequently, in order to keep chaos at bay.

Alternatively, you may just want an occasional blitz or spring-clean, in which case your best bet is to find a reliable local agency which will send round a team or individual to give your home a thorough clean-out. This is useful if dirt has got a grip and you want things like paintwork washed, light switches cleaned, kitchen cupboards turned out and so on. It can also be a lifesaver if you have got people coming to stay or want to return from holiday to find everything squeaky clean.

### Employing a cleaner

The best way to find help with cleaning is to ask around and advertise locally. Rely on personal recommendation if you can, having made searching enquiries about the two most important factors – honesty and cleaning ability. If you are considering someone without personal recommendation ask if he or she has worked for someone else and whether you can take up a telephone reference. Try to check that the referee is not a friend or relative of the applicant. If you have any concerns, look elsewhere.

Otherwise use an agency to find help for you. Agencies either charge a fee for finding the cleaner, who is then paid by you, or charge a slightly higher-than-average hourly rate if they employ the cleaner. Many people think the higher rate is worth paying as the agency will handle any problems which occur, sacking the individual or finding a replacement if misdemeanours are committed or he or she is otherwise unsatisfactory. Check what your/their position is regarding insurance.

When interviewing, show your potential employee all round your home and spell out exactly what you want done; make sure he or she is happy to do it. Many cleaners have unfavourite tasks like cleaning ovens or insides of windows, and if these chores are high on your list of priorities you will want to hire someone who is prepared to undertake them.

If you are hiring someone yourself make it quite clear what the hourly rate for the job will be. Also discuss whether you will provide some paid holiday (specifying the number of days) and what will happen if your cleaning day falls on a public holiday.

Normally, domestic cleaners are self-employed and you do not need to provide a written contract of employment. An oral agreement is sufficient. The cleaner would then be paid in cash or by cheque each time he or she worked for you. If you are taking on a cleaner as your employee, and you will be paying their National Insurance and income tax, you must provide a written contract containing the terms and conditions of employment. To find out about the National Insurance and income tax costs involved consult your local Inland Revenue office.

Next, decide whether you will let the cleaner have a key to allow access to your home when you are not in. It is worth bearing in mind that even if you are sure that your cleaner is scrupulously honest other members of his or her household may not be and may take advantage of the trust placed in your cleaner. Note, too, that if you have a burglar alarm you will have to ensure that your cleaner can switch it off – again, this is information which you may prefer to restrict to members of your household.

You should in any case inform your household contents insurer that you are employing someone to clean your home. If you do not do so, and do allow someone to have keys to your home, you may have problems claiming in the event of burglary. This information should not affect the premium although, oddly enough, insurers are more concerned about people who are in your home for long periods (e.g. a cleaner who comes in every morning) than if you just employ someone for a couple of hours a week. Their theory is that the longer people are in your home the greater the opportunity they have to steal things.

You should also tell the building insurer that you employ a cleaner, in case you are required to take out a policy for accidental damage caused by the cleaner. Also make sure you are covered in the event of your cleaner being injured while on your premises.

---

**Avoiding cowboy contractors**

Employing a cleaning contractor for a particular job requires vigilance. Unemployment has encouraged many enterprising but unqualified people to set themselves up as carpet cleaners, upholstery cleaners, curtain cleaners, dry-cleaners and so on. They may well have satisfactory equipment but they may lack training, expertise and awareness of certain problems.

Do not ever use a cleaning contractor who is either not a member of a recognised trade body or does not come with personal recommendation from someone whose opinion you trust. Tales are legion of carpets ruined with rust marks because foil wasn't put under furniture legs, upholstery ripped to shreds by steam-cleaning and designer clothes spoiled by incompetent dry-cleaning.

In the Addresses section at the back of this book are listed some trade organisations which vet their potential members and which operate a code of practice, usually drawn up in conjunction with the Office of Fair Trading. In the event of an unsatisfactory piece of work being carried out they will send round inspectors and arbitrate between the client and the contractor. This may not always result in a perfect arrangement from the client's point of view, but it is a lot better than responding to a special-offer cleaning leaflet pushed through your letterbox whose operator, after the work is done, turns out to be a fly-by-night with a PO Box address who will never respond to your complaint.

Carpets, upholstery and so on are expensive items which need care in cleaning. If you have any concerns about someone who offers to do a job for you, don't use that firm.

---

### Keeping standards up

If you can find good help with cleaning you will save yourself time and trouble. But it is important to keep your cleaner up to the mark; if the standard of work drops significantly without adequate reason you should point this out. It is also a good idea to vary the chores you set each time so that the routine does not become repetitive and dull for the cleaner. Obviously some areas (kitchen, bathrooms, etc.) need regular attention but you can vary other chores so that, for example, metal is polished one week, all the curtains are vacuumed the next, and so on.

You should also try to ensure that you are getting the time you pay for. If you cannot be at home yourself perhaps a friend could occasionally pop in to see that the cleaner has not left early or is not watching television. Since the introduction of itemised billing, you can now check if the person is using your telephone.

Checking up in this way may seem excessively cautious, but the fact is that you are employing someone to help you and make your life easier, and there is a contract between you and your cleaner, verbal or written, that confirms what both parties have agreed. In a business situation people do not put up with staff working shorter hours than specified or spending time on personal phone calls or coffee breaks. It is not unreasonable, since you are paying for your cleaner's time, to expect value for money and a professional attitude to the job.

### Au pairs

If you employ an au pair, he or she can give you some help with cleaning, although the Home Office lays down regulations about the number of hours and specifies 'light household duties' only. Au pairs may not work more than five hours a day, with at least two full days off a week, and any child-minding should be included in this total. They should also not be asked to scrub filthy floors or undertake major cleaning tasks. However, tidying up, vacuuming, dusting and polishing are all considered light duties.

Au pairs must be single and aged between 17 and 27. They can come from a number of countries specified by the Home Office (see box opposite). If you employ someone from one of these countries full-time, he or she must have a work permit. Although EU nationals are not included in the au pair scheme, they are free to take up au pair placements in the UK.

Au pairs from the following countries can work in the UK: Andorra, Bosnia-Herzegovina*, Croatia, Cyprus, Czech Republic, Faroe Islands, Greenland, Hungary, Macedonia*, Malta, Monaco, San Marino, Slovak Republic*, Slovenia, Switzerland and Turkey*.

\* Nationals of these countries must have a visa before travelling to the UK.

Unless your prospective au pair is known to you through personal recommendation (of itself, not necessarily a guarantee of satisfaction), it makes sense to go through an au pair agency rather than follow up random advertisements in local newspapers or noticeboards. Agencies bear some responsibility for the au pairs they recommend. They will take account of your circumstances (late getting home from work, say) and try to find someone who is prepared to meet your requirements (for example, perhaps you want someone who has possessed a driving licence for at least two years). They will take up references and, in the case of problems, fire the au pair and arrange for a new post or repatriation – potentially embarrassing situations given that the person is living in your home. You will obviously pay a fee for this service but it could well be offset by the convenience it offers.

# Chapter 2

# Stain removal

Basic kit for stain removal

Treatment tips

Protective measures

Specific stain treatments

It is important to make tackling stains the first step in any cleaning process. Stains become more difficult or even impossible to get out when they are not treated correctly. For example, hot water 'sets' some stains, such as blood, which may then always remain visible. Some cleaning products will rub a stain into the carpet ineradicably.

It makes sense to keep a stain removal kit in the cupboard and use the items in it only for this purpose. Otherwise, the day you want nail varnish remover you will find the bottle in the bedroom has run out.

Buy stain removers in small quantities and replace them as needed. If you decant something into another container (not advisable with some chemicals), make sure it is clearly labelled and in a suitable bottle. Products that are sold in glass containers should not be decanted into plastic.

## Basic kit for stain removal

**Acetone** (also sold as non-oily nail varnish remover)
**Ammonia**
**Biological detergent** (also called enzyme detergent)
**Bleach** (note that bleaches come in different strengths – check the instructions for the amount of water needed for dilution)
**Carpet stain remover**
**French chalk** (Fuller's earth – available from chemists – or unperfumed talcum powder)
**Glycerine**
**Grease solvents** (sold in aerosol, liquid and stick form)
**Hydrogen peroxide**
**Laundry borax**
**Methylated spirit** (do not use on acetates or triacetates – see clothing label – as it will melt them)
**Pre-wash laundry products**
**Proprietary stain removers** (these are specially formulated for particular stains such as ink, rust, tar, etc. They may be in aerosol or liquid form. See Chapter 9, Products that work)
**Soda siphon** (these are fairly easy to acquire second-hand. Alternatively, you can use bottled soda water – although the 'whoosh' factor of a siphon lends extra cleaning power)
**Surgical spirit**
**Toothbrush or nailbrush**

**White spirit** (paint thinner)
**White malt vinegar**
**White rags**
**White unpatterned kitchen paper**

## Treatment tips

- Treat stains as soon as possible – early treatment is more likely to be successful.
- Always follow the instructions supplied with a cleaning product, noting any surfaces on which it cannot be used.
- Test the cleaning product on an inconspicuous area before applying to the stain. This might be a patch of wallpaper that is always hidden by a picture, or an inside seam of a garment.
- Never mix stain-removal treatments – the chemicals may react together adversely.
- Never use coloured rags or paper napkins on stains – the chemicals can cause their colour to run.
- It may be necessary to apply a stain remover several times. This is preferable to the 'blitz' approach – e.g. using a large quantity of bleach on something.
- Pay for professional cleaning if an item is valuable or if the manufacturer recommends it. If you have already tried to treat the stain, tell the cleaner what products you have used as this may affect how he or she treats the item.
- Keep care instructions in a ring binder or box file if you have removed them from the item to which they refer.

## Protective measures

All cleaning with chemicals, whether proprietary products or basic items such as ammonia and turpentine, produces polluting fumes. Even if you work in well-ventilated conditions you may find you suffer from volatile organic chemical (VOC) syndrome (see Appendix I, Chemicals in cleaning products, for more about this).

Be sure to take the following precautions:

- Always open a window or outside door so that the area is well ventilated.
- Wear suitable gloves to protect your hands.

- Avoid getting chemicals on your skin or in your eyes. If you do, rinse thoroughly with cold water. If stinging or burning persists see your doctor or go to the accident and emergency department of your nearest hospital.
- Keep all chemicals away from naked flames. Do not smoke while you are treating a stain.
- Keep children and pets out of the way while you are working. Treat stains away from aquarium fish and caged animals if possible.

> The initial treatment for any stain is to blot it with kitchen paper or an old white towel. Solid stains should be lifted off a surface using a blunt knife or the bowl of a spoon. Work carefully from the perimeter of the stain towards the centre to prevent it spreading.

## Specific stain treatments

**Beer**    *Carpets* Freshly spilled beer on carpets and washable fabrics should come out after being sponged with warm water or squirted from a soda siphon. Shampoo the whole carpet afterwards, or you may end up with a clean patch which is just as conspicuous as a stain. Use methylated spirit on old beer stains.

*Soft furnishings and fabrics* If normal washing fails, sponge white fabrics with 20-vol strength hydrogen peroxide in a solution of six parts cold water to one of hydrogen peroxide, and coloured fabrics with a solution of 30ml white vinegar in 500ml cold water.

*Non-washable fabrics* Use an aerosol dry-cleaner.

**Beetroot**    *Washable fabrics* Rinse thoroughly in cold water, then launder in a biological detergent solution. White fabrics such as table linen can be stretched over a bowl or basin, sprinkled with laundry borax and left for 15 minutes or so. Rinse with hot water and launder according to fabric.

Coloured fabric should be soaked in a warm solution of laundry borax (15ml to 500ml water).

Scrape up with a spoon, then sponge with warm water or a laundry borax solution.

**Bird droppings**

*Carpets* You may need to use a proprietary stain remover.

*Non-washable fabrics and upholstery* Use an aerosol stain remover.

*Washable fabrics* Droppings which fall on laundry hanging out to dry should come out with a normal re-wash. Droppings which contain berry stains may require diluted bleach (for white fabrics) or (for coloured fabrics) a solution of 20-vol hydrogen peroxide (one part to six parts cold water). Take care with coloured fabrics – test the effect first by dabbing a little peroxide solution on an unobtrusive area.

If a lot of blood has been spilled it may smell. Use a pet stain and odour remover to get rid of this.

**Blood**

*Carpets* Spray the stain with a soda siphon, then sponge with plain cold water.

*Washable fabrics* Soak in cold water containing a handful of salt. Then soak in a solution of biological detergent and launder as usual.

*Non-washable fabrics* Sponge with a solution of ammonia (2.5ml to 1 litre cold water). Rinse with cold water and immediately pat dry with kitchen paper.

Blood on a mattress requires a thick paste of bicarbonate of soda (use as little water as possible). Stand the mattress on its side so that little water gets into it. When the paste is dry brush it off. Repeat this process until the stain goes. Finally, sponge with cold salty water.

**Candle wax**  **Hard surfaces** Scrape up as much as you can using the bowl of a spoon. Put a plastic bag of ice cubes on the wax to harden it, then chip it off. Take a medium-hot iron and apply it to the remains of the stain *over a piece of white blotting paper.* (You can use brown paper but it is less absorbent; kitchen paper is too thin and the heat from the iron may damage the surface below.)

For wood surfaces in particular, make sure the blotting paper is large enough to prevent the iron touching the wood, and keep the iron on the lowest setting possible to melt the wax.

**Other materials** Scrape off, then use a stain remover on fabrics and wall coverings; methylated spirit on carpets.

**Car and cycle oil**  Use white spirit on concrete garage floors and driveways. Use a solution of sugar soap on asphalt. (See also 'Drives', page 172.)

**Carbon paper**  Use either a stain remover or methylated spirit.

**Chalk (blackboard)**  Will wash out of washable fabrics. On hard surfaces, brush off loose chalk then wipe with a solution of washing-up-liquid.

**Chewing gum**  **Carpets and upholstery** Use a special chewing-gum remover (available in most supermarkets).

**Clothes** Fill a plastic bag with ice cubes or put the garment in the freezer (in a plastic bag) so that the gum hardens and can be chipped off. If necessary, use lighter fuel, applied (with caution) on a cloth. Use a liquid stain remover on any remaining marks. Launder or sponge with warm water.

**Chocolate**  Scrape up as much as possible.

**Carpets, upholstery and non-washable fabrics** Use a proprietary stain remover.

**Washable fabrics** Launder in biological detergent.

***Carpets*** Blot up as much as possible, then squirt with a soda siphon and pat dry. This should remove fresh black coffee but white coffee leaves a grease mark, which should be treated with a solution of carpet shampoo or a carpet spot removal kit. Dried coffee stains should be given the soda siphon treatment several times, allowing it to dry between applications.

***Non-washable fabrics and upholstery*** Sponge first with laundry borax solution (15ml borax to 500ml warm water), then with clear water. Where marks persist, use a stain remover.

***Washable fabrics*** Rinse in warm water then soak in a biological detergent solution or a laundry borax solution. Launder as usual and use a stain remover to lift any traces.

*Coffee*

Put the stained garments through another cycle, using a special dye remover designed for machine use. Soaking laundry in a biological detergent solution may help. A bleach solution will deal with white fabrics.

*Colour run in laundry load*

Allow the fluid to dry and with your nails or a blunt knife pick off as much as possible. On **carpets** and **upholstery** you may need to shampoo or call in a professional if the stain is bad (see page 85). Once picked off, the fluid should wash out of clothes. Anything that needs dry-cleaning should be cleaned professionally – be sure to tell the cleaner what the mark is.

If correction fluid on a document gets on to the flatbed of a **photocopier**, use methylated spirit to remove it. Never scrape the flatbed.

*Correction fluid*

Treat foundation cream, lipstick, eyeshadow and mascara with white spirit, then launder the items or sponge them with warm water.

Spilled nail varnish should be blotted well, then removed with non-oily nail varnish remover.

*Cosmetics*

**Crayon**    *Wallpaper* If the damage covers a smallish space the only solution is to fix a patch. Tear it to an irregular shape so that the edges will not look quite so obvious. This is quite successful with patterned paper but tends to be a bit obvious with plain papers. For large areas, try the Helping Hands Giant Dry-Cleaning Pad (see Chapter 9, Products that work).
*Vinyl wallcoverings and bedheads* Use a household cleaner and rinse. Restore sheen by buffing well with a soft cloth. Marks on vinyl can often be removed with milk.
*Fabrics* Crayon will either wash out or can be removed with a grease solvent.

**Creosote**    *Washable fabrics* Hold a pad of white cloth on top of the stain and dab liquid lighter fuel or eucalyptus oil from underneath to push the stain into the pad. Old stains should first be softened by covering with a solution of glycerine and warm water (equal parts) left on for an hour or so, then rinsed out. Launder according to fabric type.
*Non-washable fabrics* These should be dry-cleaned professionally. Call in a specialist carpet cleaner if necessary.

**Curry**    Curry produces a tricky stain which should be removed professionally from garments or furnishings that you value. Otherwise scrape up as much as possible and treat as follows.
*Carpets and non-washable fabrics* Sponge with a laundry borax solution (15ml to 500ml warm water), then with clean water and pat dry. Treat remaining marks with a stain remover.
*Washable fabrics* Soak in warm water, changing it if necessary. Squeeze out as much water as possible and apply a solution of equal parts glycerine and warm water. Leave for at least an hour then rinse with clear water. Repeat if necessary. Launder using biological detergent. White items can be treated with a bleach solution.

**Dye**

**Carpets, non-washable fabrics and upholstery**
Sponge with methylated spirit (not on acetates or triacetates) to which a few drops of household ammonia have been added. Repeat if necessary. Have valuable items dry-cleaned professionally. (See 'Dry-cleaning', Chapter 5.)

**Hard surfaces** Mop up immediately with a dry cloth. Do not use water as it will spread the dye. Dye that has dried in cannot be removed.

**Washable fabrics** Soak in a biological detergent solution, then launder as usual. On white washable fabrics use a proprietary dye stripper, following the instructions supplied. Silk and wool can be soaked in a 20-vol hydrogen peroxide solution (one part to six parts cold water) for a maximum of 15 minutes. Rinse immediately and launder by hand. Always soak the whole item in case of colour change.

**Egg**

Scrape up as much as possible, rubbing gently with kitchen paper to loosen the mark. Raw egg should be mopped up and then sponged with cold salty water. Cooked egg is less of a problem because it tends to be more easily scooped up. Remove what you can with a spoon, then treat the stain according to the cooking method. Boiled egg can usually be wiped up with warm water or a weak solution of washing-up liquid. Cooked egg that involves grease, such as poached, scrambled or fried, will probably need the application of a grease solvent and, in the cases of carpet or upholstery, an appropriate shampoo. Be very careful not to apply any hot liquid as egg sets fast and then becomes difficult to remove.

**Carpets** Use a carpet spotting kit or proprietary stain remover, then shampoo the carpet. Use an aerosol stain remover on raw egg stains.

**Non-washable fabrics and upholstery** Sponge with cold salty water, then with plain water. Use an upholstery shampoo on any remaining marks.
**Washable fabrics** Soak in cold salty water then rinse. Soak in plain water then launder. Raw egg should be removed using biological detergent.

**Faeces** Baby and pet accidents can occur in even the best-run homes. Treat immediately as for vomit (see page 47).

**Flowers** Stains can result from the pollen from flower stamens – lilies are the worst.
**Fabrics and upholstery** Dab flower stains with methylated spirit (but not on acetates or triacetates), sponge with warm water and, if possible, launder.
**Wallcoverings** Brush off as much as possible and use an aerosol or liquid stain remover applied with a cotton bud. Try to prevent flowerheads, especially stamens, touching walls.
**Vases and bowls** Marks can be removed by soaking the vessel in a weak bleach solution for 30 minutes.

**Flying insects** **Upholstery** Use an aerosol stain remover or methylated spirit (but not on acetates and triacetates).
**Fabric lampshades** Brush thoroughly but gently with a soft brush, then use an aerosol stain remover.
**Plastic and vellum lampshades** Wipe with a cloth dampened in a solution of soapflakes. Sponge off with clear water and leave to dry.

**Fruit juice** Blot immediately with kitchen paper or a white towel.
**Carpets and upholstery** Sponge with warm water and then shampoo. Remaining colour stains should be dabbed with methylated spirit.

*Washable fabrics* Rinse in cold running water. Stretch table and bed linen over a bowl or sink and pour hot water through the stain. Squeeze out water and cover marks with a glycerine solution (equal parts glycerine and warm water). Launder items according to their fabric.
*Non-washable fabrics* Sponge with cold water and allow to dry naturally. Then use a proprietary stain remover.

**Glue**

Treat by scraping up as much as possible and then use an appropriate solvent. Adhesives manufacturers produce solvents specifically designed to remove glue spills. Buy the solvent at the same time as the glue in case of spillage.
*Carpets* Stains on pile carpets that will not come off can be removed by snipping the pile slightly with very sharp embroidery scissors. This may be essential if a carpet has a built-in foam backing which could be dissolved by stain remover or solvent. Use non-oily nail varnish remover on clear adhesives; paint-thinner on epoxy resin; liquid grease solvent on latex adhesive.
*Hard surfaces* Use white or methylated spirit to remove sticky label residue, except on bare metal, on which nail varnish remover should do the trick. Allow latex adhesives to set, then roll them off with your finger.

**Grass**

*Washable fabrics* Stains should come out when the article is laundered. If marks remain, dab with methylated spirit (but not on acetates or triacetates) and rinse.
*Non-washable fabrics* Cover the stain with a mixture of cream of tartar powder and fine salt (equal parts), leave for 15 minutes and brush dry. Dry-clean.

**Hair dye**  Henna is a particularly difficult dye to remove. Treat any spills immediately by wiping with a white cloth and warm (not hot) water. Persistent and old stains will never come out.

*White cotton* Dilute one cupful of household ammonia in a gallon of warm water and pour it directly on to the stain, allowing it to drain through. If the stain is not shifting, soak the item in the solution for up to four hours. Rinse, wash in hot water, and allow to dry naturally.

*Coloured or manmade fabrics* Test the effect on a hidden area before proceeding as for white cotton, but without allowing the item to soak.

**Hair spray**  *Washable fabrics* Wash normally.

*Non-washable fabrics* Treat with a stain remover.

*Mirrors* Wipe with a cloth dampened with methylated spirit.

**Ice-cream**  Scrape up as much as possible, then treat as follows.

*Carpets* Wipe with a damp cloth, then use a carpet spotting kit or shampoo the carpet. If grease marks remain, use a stain remover, first checking that the carpet is not foam-backed.

*Non-washable fabrics* Use a proprietary stain remover, then bleach out any colour with a solution of 20-vol hydrogen peroxide (one part to six parts cold water).

*Washable fabrics* Soak in a warm solution of biological detergent (use ordinary detergent if the fabric is not suitable). Launder at the highest temperature the fabric can take even if it means washing the item on its own. Silk and wool should never be soaked, so sponge with a warm solution of laundry borax (15ml to 500ml water) then sponge immediately with warm water.

Inks are difficult to remove and some old ink stains will never come out of certain surfaces.

**Ink**

*Carpets* Ballpoint ink should be dried up as quickly as possible using cotton buds and kitchen paper. Dab with methylated spirit or use a proprietary stain remover. Some ballpoint pen manufacturers recommend products for removing their ink, so if this treatment does not work ask them for advice.

For fountain-pen ink stains, squirt with a soda siphon to dilute the stain then mop with kitchen paper or an old white towel. Make up a hot solution of soapflakes and apply as a poultice on a white fabric pad. Leave for at least 15 minutes, then blot and repeat until the marks disappear. Rinse with clear water. For bad marks use a carpet spotting kit and possibly a carpet shampoo.

Blot felt-tip pen stains with cotton buds and kitchen paper, then dab with methylated spirit.

*Non-washable fabrics* Use a proprietary stain remover on felt-tip or fountain pen stains.

*Washable fabrics* White fabrics can be treated with household bleach. Keep ink stains damp using cold water until you have finished treatment. Dried ink is much harder to remove.

*Vinyl wallcoverings* Scrub ballpoint ink stains with a stiff nailbrush dipped into a solution of washing-up liquid. Use a non-abrasive household cleaner on felt-tip pen marks, then clean with a solution of washing-up liquid and rinse off. Use an aerosol vinyl cleaner to restore shine. Milk may also be effective in removing ink from vinyl.

*Washable fabrics* Squirt or dab with lemon juice (any kind, including that sold in bottles or plastic containers) and cover with a thin layer of fine salt. Leave for an hour, rinse in cold water

**Iron mould and rust marks**

and launder as usual. Large white articles, such as sheets, which are heavily marked, can be washed using a dye remover.

*Non-washable fabrics* Treat persistent stains with a proprietary rust remover and then rinse or sponge it off.

**Jam, chutney and other preserves**

Scrape up as much as possible with the bowl of a spoon.

*Carpets* Wipe with a damp cloth several times then use a carpet shampoo. Coloured marks should be treated with methylated spirit.

*Non-washable fabrics* Sponge with a solution of washing-up liquid, blot dry with kitchen paper and repeat if necessary. Rinse with clear water. Any remaining marks should be covered with a layer of laundry borax powder, left for 15 minutes, then sponged. Otherwise use a proprietary stain remover.

*Washable fabrics* Soak in a laundry borax solution (15ml borax to 500ml warm water) before laundering.

**Mayonnaise**

*Carpets and non-washable fabrics* Wipe with a damp cloth, working into the stain to avoid spreading it. When dry use an aerosol stain remover. Carpets may need an application of shampoo.

*Table linen and washable fabrics* Sponge with warm water (hot water will set the egg content and make it harder to remove). Soak in a biological detergent solution, then launder as usual.

Mayonnaise on expensive or 'difficult' fabric garments will need professional dry-cleaning.

**Medicine**

Sponge with warm water, then launder, using methylated spirit to remove any trace of colour. If a stain looks particularly sinister ask your local pharmacist what is in the medicine and how to treat the mark.

### Metal polish

Spoon and blot up as much as possible.

**Carpets** Dab the stain with methylated spirit and let it dry naturally. Beat with a stiff hand-brush to loosen the powdery residue, then vacuum it up. Shampoo after vacuuming if necessary.

**Washable fabrics** Use a proprietary stain remover, then launder.

**Non-washable fabrics** Sponge and leave to dry then brush thoroughly with a stiff clothes-brush (which you will need to clean afterwards). Use a proprietary stain remover on any remaining marks.

### Mildew

Mildew is a growth of spores, which continue to develop if left unchecked. It is generally fairly easy to remove with a solution of bleach.

Mildew in the **bathroom**, especially around the edge of a shower tray, needs a special sealant cleaner applied at fairly frequent intervals – unless you can train the people in your household to wipe the shower tray dry after each use. Use a toothbrush to get into awkward corners.

The mildew that builds up on the **putty around glass** in windows can be cleaned with bleach or a fungicide. Use a cotton bud to get into awkward corners and narrow spaces.

Where mildew builds up on **flat roofs** or **patios**, use a strong garden paving cleaner. Work on a small area at a time and hose off thoroughly. Make sure that the cleaning product does not get on to lawns or flower beds.

**Non-washable fabrics and upholstery** Brush spores off (outdoors if possible), then spray with an anti-mildew solution to kill any that remain. Some items may need dry-cleaning.

Take professional advice from a local museum if mildew has attacked any valuable textiles.

***Washable fabrics*** Laundering is usually sufficient. On white fabrics (apart from nylon) mildew should be bleached with a 20-vol hydrogen peroxide solution (one part to six parts cold water). Household bleach is suitable for white cottons and linens which are not treated or have a specific finish. On coloured fabrics dampen the affected areas and rub with a block of hard household soap. Leave to dry in the sun or, in winter, by the sunniest window. Launder as usual.

***Walls*** Wash with a mild detergent (for method, see page 101), then paint over a solution of proprietary bactericide. It is always worth applying bactericide before you redecorate a room with new wallcovering as this reduces the risk of mildew.

***Plastic shower curtains*** Sponge with a weak solution of household bleach or antiseptic. This should clear light marking, but bad marks should be treated with a detergent solution then rinsed with proprietary bactericide.

Many shower curtains are now washable, and you can also buy mildew-resistant ones.

***Leather*** Sponge with a mild solution of household disinfectant (5ml to 500ml warm water). If applying to shoes, be sure to cover the whole of both shoes. Wipe dry and buff with a soft cloth. Apply a thin layer of hide food (shoe polish on shoes).

**Milk** Do not leave spilled milk to dry: the smell becomes virtually ineradicable. For this reason it is particularly important to treat immediately milk spilled in cars. Squirt with a soda siphon or lukewarm water (not even hand-hot as this will set the stain) and blot thoroughly with kitchen paper.

*Carpets* Use a carpet shampoo followed by a stain remover if marks remain.

*Non-washable fabrics and upholstery* Sponge with lukewarm water then use a stain remover.

*Washable fabrics* Rinse in lukewarm water then soak in a biological detergent solution. Launder as appropriate.

Mud should always be allowed to dry so that **Mud** you can brush off as much as possible with a stiff handbrush or vacuum cleaner tool before taking any further action.

*Carpets* Use a carpet shampoo followed by methylated spirit on any colour traces left by the mud.

*Non-washable fabrics and upholstery* Sponge with a warm solution of washing-up liquid, rinse with clear water and blot thoroughly.

*Washable fabrics and clothing (not waterproofs)* Brush dried mud off, use a stain remover on bad marks, then launder as usual.

Powder and made-up mustards require the **Mustard** same treatment, although if you are having an item dry-cleaned you should tell the cleaner exactly what type of mustard it is – many contain extra flavourings that may affect treatment.

*Washable fabrics* Soak the stained area in a weak detergent solution, then sponge with a solution of ammonia (5ml to 500ml warm water). Launder as usual. Stains which have dried should be covered with a glycerine solution (equal parts glycerine and warm water) for an hour or so before rinsing and laundering.

*Non-washable fabrics* Dry-cleaning is the best treatment, but you can sponge with a weak solution of detergent then dab remaining marks with an ammonia solution (5ml to 500ml warm water). Blot, then sponge with clear water. Do not apply this treatment to any fabric that will ringmark.

**Nicotine**  For nicotine stains on the skin, apply neat sterilising fluid (for babies' bottles) on a pad of cotton wool, then wash off.

If there are heavy smokers in your home you will find that paintwork gradually becomes discoloured, particularly on ceilings above a favourite smoking spot. Washing with a cleaning product may help but you will usually have to resign yourself to regular repainting jobs.

**Oil, fat and grease**  (See also 'Car and cycle oil', page 28 and 'Paraffin oil', page 42.)

*Carpets*  Lay a pad of white blotting paper over the stain and apply a medium-hot iron to draw the grease into the paper. Take care not to damage any foam backing. Make up a strong solution of carpet shampoo and rub the lather into the marks. Wipe off with kitchen paper and repeat the shampoo treatment until the marks disappear. Even when you think you have cleared a grease stain it may reappear days or weeks later as it works its way up the carpet pile. If it does, repeat the treatment.

---

If you spill fat on to fabric or a carpet and don't have a grease solvent handy, sprinkle talcum powder on it and brush or vacuum it up when it has absorbed the fat. You may need to repeat the treatment.

---

*Non-washable fabrics and upholstery*  Sprinkle on a layer of talcum powder or Fuller's earth; as it absorbs the grease wipe or brush off and re-apply. Leave the final layer for several hours then brush off. Alternatively, use the blotting paper/iron treatment (see 'Candle wax', page 28) followed by a stain remover.

**Washable fabrics** Launder in the hottest water possible. On delicate fabrics and wool, dab with eucalyptus oil, then sponge or launder as appropriate.

**Leather shoes, upholstery and handbags** Oil can sometimes be wiped off before it sinks in. If it stains, cover the marks with a layer of bicycle puncture repair adhesive (having first checked on a test area that colour will not be affected). Leave it on for 24 hours, then peel off carefully. Apply shoe polish or hide food. Oil on a suede coat can sometimes be removed with the brush or block supplied. If this does not work have the garment cleaned professionally. For suede shoes blot with a tissue, then rub with a block cleaner. If this fails rub a little lighter fuel on the stain with a ball of cotton wool. If colour is affected you will need to treat the whole of both shoes.

## Paint

Always treat while still fresh if possible. Dried paint is much harder to remove.

**Acrylic** Blot quickly with kitchen paper and wash in soapy water. Where a stain has dried put a pad of white cloth underneath it and dab with methylated spirit or a liquid grease solvent.

**Oil paint** Hold a pad of white cloth underneath and dab with white spirit, then sponge or launder. Hardened oil paint may respond to a liquid stain remover.

**Poster, powder and water colours** Sponge or soak in cold water. Launder garments; shampoo carpets and upholstery.

**Emulsion and other water-based paint** On carpets and upholstery, mop up and blot as much as possible, sponge with cold water and treat with a carpet/upholstery shampoo. Professional cleaning may be needed. If stains have dried soften them with methylated spirit (but not on acetates and triacetates) before treatment. On non-washable fabrics dried stains are best dry-cleaned.

***Gloss and other oil-based paint*** Spoon up as much as possible and dab any residue with white spirit or a stain remover. Rinse with clean water and repeat.

**Paraffin oil**   Blot quickly with kitchen paper.

***Carpets*** Use an aerosol stain remover (call in professional cleaners if a large area is stained).

***Non-washable and washable fabrics*** See 'Oil, fat and grease', page 40.

**Perfume**   ***Washable fabrics*** Rinse immediately. Cover dried stains with a glycerine solution (equal parts glycerine and warm water). Leave for an hour or more, then launder.

***Non-washable fabrics*** Leave a glycerine solution on for an hour, then wipe over with a warm damp cloth and pat dry. Have expensive clothes cleaned professionally. Put perfume on *before* you dress.

**Perspiration**   ***Washable fabrics*** Sponge with a solution of ammonia (5ml to 500ml warm water). Rinse immediately. Where colour has altered, sponge with a solution of white vinegar (15ml to 250ml warm water) and rinse before laundering. If appropriate for the fabric, soak in a biological detergent solution; otherwise launder as usual. Bleach marks out of white garments (other than nylon) with a solution of 20-vol hydrogen peroxide (one part to six parts cold water).

***Non-washable fabrics*** Dab marks with a solution of white vinegar (15ml to 250ml warm water), which will also reduce any smell. Where colour has been affected, rub with methylated spirit (but not on acetates or triacetates – men's suits are frequently lined with these and should be cleaned professionally).

**Plasticine and playdough**

Scrape up with a blunt knife. Use ice cubes on any residue to make it easier to chip off. If possible put an absorbent pad under the stain and dab with a liquid stain remover to get rid of the deposit. Any remaining colour can be treated with methylated spirit. Launder washable fabrics, sponge non-washables and shampoo carpets and upholstery.

**Rust**

See 'Iron mould and rust', page 35.

**Scorch marks**

*Carpets* Beat with a stiff brush to remove loose pile. If a mark is not too bad the easiest solution may be to simply trim off the top of the pile using sharp embroidery scissors. Otherwise use a piece of coarse glasspaper and sand with a circular movement until the mark has disappeared or become less obvious. For bad scorch marks you may need to patch the area with an offcut, using a sharp knife and double-sided tape. Ensure that the pile of the offcut runs the same way as that of the rest of the carpet.

*Non-washable fabrics* Use a glycerine solution (equal parts glycerine and water) left on for an hour. Sponge off with warm water. A laundry borax solution (15ml to 500ml warm water) can fade bad marks: follow by sponging with clear water and repeat the treatment if necessary.

*Washable fabrics* Rub marks with your fingers under cold running water, then soak the item in a laundry borax solution. Rinse and launder. Bad marks may never come out, although on suitable white fabrics (not nylon), bleaching with a solution of 20-vol hydrogen peroxide (one part to six parts cold water) may do the trick.

**Shoe polish** Scrape up as much as possible.
*Carpets, upholstery and non-washable fabrics*
Apply methylated spirit to marks, then use carpet or upholstery shampoo. A carpet spotting kit may prove useful.
*Washable fabrics* Use a stain remover or a few drops of ammonia in the rinse water when laundering. Treat bad marks with white spirit before washing.

**Soot marks** *Bricks* Brush well or use a vacuum cleaner attachment. Scrub marks using a hard scrubbing brush and clean water. If this fails, apply neat malt vinegar on a cloth or brush and then rinse thoroughly. Heavy staining should be treated with a solution of spirit of salts (one part to six parts cold water). Spirit of salts is corrosive, toxic and gives off poisonous fumes. Protect yourself suitably, open windows and ensure the solution does not come into contact with the pointing between the bricks. Rinse thoroughly with warm water.
*Stonework* Scrub with clear water, then use a mild solution of washing-up liquid on remaining marks. Bad stains may respond to an application of neat household bleach. Rinse well.

**Spirits (alcoholic)** *Carpets and upholstery* Blot up as much as possible and squirt the area with a soda siphon. If stains remain, use a carpet spotting kit or apply the lather of a carpet or upholstery shampoo. Dried-in spirit stains may respond to methylated spirit.
*Non-washable fabrics* Sponge with warm water and blot dry. Treat stains with a solution of washing-up liquid applied on a cloth. Wipe over with a clean wet cloth.
*Washable fabrics* Rinse in warm water and wash as usual.

Scrape up what you can, taking care not to damage carpet or fabric. **Tar**

**Carpets and non-washable fabrics** Apply a glycerine solution (equal parts glycerine and water) to the marks and leave for an hour. Rinse with clear water. Use a carpet spotting kit or proprietary stain remover, then rinse with cold water.

**Washable fabrics** Put an absorbent white pad on top of the mark and apply eucalyptus oil on a cotton wool pad from below. Wash as usual.

**Shoes** Use lighter fuel, checking first on an inconspicuous part that colour will not be affected.

Treat as soon as possible, particularly if it contains milk. **Tea**

**Carpets** Mop up as much as possible and squirt with a soda siphon or clean with warm water. Use a carpet shampoo if the tea contained milk and then treat remaining stains with a stain remover. Dried marks should be sponged with a laundry borax solution (15ml to 500ml warm water) and rinsed. If marks remain, cover with a glycerine solution (equal parts glycerine and water), leave for an hour, then sponge off with clear water. Use a carpet shampoo.

**Non-washable fabrics and upholstery** Wipe over with a laundry borax solution (15ml laundry borax to 500ml warm water) then sponge with clear water. Pat well to remove moisture and when dry use an aerosol stain remover or upholstery spotting kit.

**Washable fabrics** Rinse in warm water and soak in a laundry borax solution (15ml to 500ml warm water) or biological detergent solution. Soften dried stains with a glycerine solution for an hour. Launder as usual.

Tablecloths should be rinsed under cold running water, then soaked in a biological detergent solution. Cloths with dry tea stains should be stretched over a bowl or basin and covered with laundry borax powder. Pour hot water through, then wash as usual. White fabrics can be cleaned with household bleach.

Tea spilled in bed on blankets should be rinsed out in warm water before the blankets are laundered.

**Tomato ketchup and other bottled sauces** Spoon and blot up as much as possible, taking care not to spread the stain.

*Carpets* Sponge with warm water and blot well. Apply lather from made-up carpet shampoo, wiping in the direction of the pile. Wipe over with a damp cloth. When dry use a stain remover on remaining marks.

*Non-washable fabrics and upholstery* Use a spoon or blunt knife to remove as much of the deposit as possible. Wipe over with a damp cloth, allow to dry and apply a proprietary stain remover. Tomato-based sauces are notoriously difficult to clean and may require professional treatment.

*Washable fabrics* Rinse the stained area in running cold water. Sponge with a soapflake solution and rinse well. Appropriate fabrics can be soaked in a biological detergent solution. Launder according to fabric.

**Urine** *Carpets* Squirt with a soda siphon and blot well with kitchen paper. Wipe over the area two or three times with cold water to which you have added a few drops of antiseptic. You can also buy a special carpet cleaner which contains deodorant. Remove dried urine stains by sponging with an ammonia solution (2.5ml to 500ml cold water).

*Non-washable fabrics* Sponge with cold water and blot well. Remove any remaining stains with a solution of white vinegar (15ml to 500ml warm water). Dried stains will need professional attention. You can get rid of the smell with a pet stain and odour remover (see Chapter 9, Products that work).

*Washable fabrics* Rinse first in cold water, then launder as usual according to fabric. Old, dried stains should be soaked in a biological detergent solution. Marks on appropriate white fabrics (not nylon) can be bleached with a solution of 20-vol hydrogen peroxide (one part to six parts cold water) with a few drops of ammonia added.

*Mattresses* Turn the mattress on its side to prevent water penetration. Hold a towel below the stain with one hand while you sponge the area with a cold solution of washing-up liquid or upholstery shampoo. Wipe over with clear water containing a few drops of antiseptic or sterilising fluid. Leave to dry thoroughly before returning to position. A mark will probably remain but the smell will have gone as will the urine chemicals which could otherwise rot the mattress's cover fabric. If any smell does remain, use a pet stain and odour remover.

*Shoes* Urine on leather shoes should be wiped off immediately with tissue paper and the area buffed up. For suede shoes, rub marks with a cloth wrung out in clean warm water; while the shoes are still damp apply a suede brush to raise the nap. Dried marks may respond to a special shoe stain remover.

## Vomit

Scrape up as much deposit as possible.

*Carpets* Flush with a soda siphon and blot well. Rub in the lather from a made-up solution of carpet shampoo; apply several times if necessary. Rinse with warm water to which you have added a few drops of antiseptic or use a carpet shampoo with a built-in deodorant.

**Non-washable fabrics** Clear as much as possible, then sponge the fabric with warm water containing a few drops of ammonia. Blot dry. Use a pet stain and odour remover (see Chapter 9, Products that work) to get rid of any smell. Have delicate fabrics and expensive garments dry-cleaned professionally.

**Washable fabrics** Clear the deposit and rinse the fabric under cold running water. If suitable, soak and wash in a biological detergent solution; otherwise launder as usual.

**Mattresses** Turn the mattress on its side and, holding a towel below the stain with one hand, sponge the affected area with a warm solution of washing-up liquid or an upholstery shampoo. Wipe over with cold water containing a few drops of antiseptic. Blot well. Use a pet stain and odour remover if necessary.

**Water marks**   **Fabrics, suede and leather** Water marks are caused by the deposit of minerals from the water on to the fabric. Gentle scratching with a fingernail will sometimes remove them. Otherwise, hold the fabric in front of a steaming kettle spout for a few minutes, then, as it dries, rub the mark from the edge towards the centre. This treatment is not suitable for silk or chiffon.

**Wine**   **Carpets** Fresh red wine stains will disappear when white wine is poured on them, but there are cheaper solutions: squirt a soda siphon on the stain and blot well. Apply the lather from made-up carpet shampoo two or three times, then wipe with a cloth wrung out in clean water. Blot well. Cover remaining traces with a glycerine solution (equal parts glycerine and water) and leave for an hour. Rinse with clear water and pat dry. Old red wine stains may come out with an application of methylated spirit. Sprinkling salt on to wine stains on carpets is an old wives' remedy; it creates a damp patch that never dries out and always attracts dirt to the area. It is, however, a useful tip for preventing a wine stain from spreading over table linen.

*Non-washable fabrics and upholstery* Blot with kitchen paper, then sponge with warm water and blot again. Cover remaining stains with Fuller's earth or talcum powder while still damp. Brush off after 10 minutes and apply another layer. Repeat applications until stain is lifted. Old dried stains should be covered with a glycerine solution (equal parts glycerine and water) left on for 30 minutes. Wipe over with clear water and if necessary use an upholstery spotting kit.

*Washable fabrics* Rinse in warm water and, if stains remain, soak in a laundry borax solution (15ml to 500ml warm water) or a biological detergent solution where suitable. Apply bleach to white fabrics with suitable finishes and use a solution of 20-vol hydrogen peroxide (one part to six parts cold water) on stained silk and wool.

Chapter 3

# General household cleaning

The kitchen

The bathroom

Beds and bedding

Carpets and rugs

Floors

Upholstery

Curtains

Blinds

Walls and ceilings

Fireplaces

## The kitchen

For reasons of hygiene, the kitchen should be kept clean at all times. This is particularly difficult if your kitchen doubles as a laundry room; try not to sort your dirty washing on the worktops. If your pets ever walk on the surfaces in the kitchen (this should be discouraged), always prepare food on chopping boards.

**Worktops** Kitchen surfaces should be kept clean and dry at all times. Wash them after preparing food, using a cleaner containing bactericide, and dry with kitchen paper.

*Corian* This is a very expensive material and should be cleaned only with materials recommended by the manufacturer. Instructions will be provided at the time of fitting.

*Laminated surfaces* These are fairly tough but you should not chop food or put hot dishes down on them. Wash and dry normally, and remove stains with undiluted washing-up liquid or a non-abrasive household cleaner. Use abrasive creams only on very persistent stains. Clean smeary surfaces with a soft cloth dipped in white vinegar.

*Textured-finish laminated surfaces* These attract dirt and need frequent cleaning. Do not scrape at ingrained dirt but use a solution of washing-up liquid and a washing-up brush to remove it, scrubbing in a circular motion. Dark colours will need careful rinsing to avoid cleaning fluid remaining in the indentations.

*Tiled surfaces* On heavily stained tiles use neat vinegar or a solution of household cleaner. Rinse and wipe dry. Watch out for food deposits which become lodged in the grouting. Clean regularly with an old toothbrush dipped in a solution of household bleach.

---

Keep cookery books clean either by standing them in a special rack or by placing them in a clear plastic bag.

---

When washing up in a sink, use a plastic bowl to protect the surface. Swill out the sink before putting in the bowl, as any trapped dirt or grit could scratch the surface of the sink.

*Sinks*

Keep the plughole clean at all times, using a bottle brush. Pour a little washing soda solution down the plughole at regular intervals (see below), taking care to avoid the surface of the sink. Leave for a couple of minutes, then rinse away.

**Acrylic sinks** These should be cared for with a cream cleaner; an application of white vinegar or lemon juice should remove stains.

---

**Blocked sinks**

Never put any solid matter down plugholes. Things like tiny bits of potato peelings can build up and cause blocking, while liquid fat, which seems to disappear miraculously, will solidify and do the same. If your sink becomes blocked follow the advice below.

- Bale out as much water as possible, then pour down a solution of washing soda (one handful to a kettleful of boiling water). Be careful of splashes – wear a plastic apron to protect clothes.
- If this does not work, stuff a rag into the overflow and place a sink plunger (available from hardware shops) over the plughole, having first greased the rim with petroleum jelly.
- Pump the plunger up and down a few times. This should build up enough pressure in the pipe to remove the blockage.

If you are still unsuccessful, put a bucket under the sink and unscrew the U-bend. Water will pour into the bucket and the blockage should be released at the same time. If not, use a straightened wire coat-hanger to poke around in the pipe and locate the blockage.

---

*Fireclay sinks and vitreous enamel sinks* These should be cleaned with a suitable bath-cleaning product (see 'Enamel', page 126).

*Stainless steel sinks* These should be rinsed and dried at the end of each day to prevent water spotting. Remove grease and surface soiling with undiluted washing-up liquid. Never use abrasive cleaners or scouring pads. Polish with a proprietary sink cleaner or a stainless steel polish, rinse and dry.

**Cookers** A wipe over with a damp cloth from time to time is usually sufficient for cooker exteriors. Clean off spills with washing-up liquid or household cleaner – apply while still warm and marks will come off more easily.

*Cooker hobs* These should be wiped over when you finish cooking. **Radiant** and **solid electric rings** usually burn themselves clean. **Solid hotplates** may need cleaning with a cream cleaner or scouring pad; when clean they should be wiped over with a few drops of vegetable oil applied on kitchen paper to prevent rust developing.

**Ceramic and halogen hobs** should be cleaned with the product recommended by the manufacturer. Take care not to scratch the surface of glass-topped hobs as the scratch marks will be impossible to remove. Always use smooth-based saucepans and wipe the bases before putting them on the hob. Make sure that any cloth used for wiping the hob is free of grit. Wipe up any sticky spills immediately, otherwise the sugar in them will crystallise and cause pitting on the surface; for other spills, wait for the hob to cool.

Some parts of **gas hobs** may be removable. These should be cleaned from time to time by immersion in a hot solution of washing-up liquid, using a nylon cleaning pad to remove encrusted dirt. Alternatively, it may be possible to clean them in the dishwasher. Use a mild abrasive cleaner on stubborn stains. Mop up spills as soon as they occur, otherwise they will form a burnt deposit that is difficult to remove.

*Cooker hoods* The filter should be changed regularly and the hood washed thoroughly in a hot solution of washing-up liquid. Built-up grease can be removed with the back of a knife blade.

*Grill pans* These should be washed each time you use them, otherwise the build-up of dripped fat can become a fire hazard. Most grill pans can be washed in a dishwasher (check the handbook). Although this is a rather extravagant use of space, it is a lot easier and more effective than washing by hand. If you do not have a dishwasher, wash in a hot solution of washing-up liquid, using a stiff brush to get rid of any burnt-on débris.

*Ovens* These should be cleaned according to type. Untreated linings should be cleaned with a suitable liquid or paste cleaner (see 'Enamel', page 126), applied on a nylon cleaning pad. Future soiling can be prevented by covering the floor and side panels of the oven with a thin paste of bicarbonate of soda and water. During cooking this dries and absorbs grease, which can be wiped out easily afterwards – particularly helpful if you are roasting.

In theory, ovens with continuous clean linings clean themselves – provided you cook fairly often at a reasonably high temperature to ensure that fat is vaporised and not deposited. Wipe over with a damp cloth after cooking and always wipe up any spills on the floor of the oven.

**Glass oven doors** should always be cleaned when cool; the effect of a cold cleaner on warm glass can cause cracking. Light soiling can be tackled with a solution of washing-up liquid; for heavier dirt apply a paste or liquid cleaner on a nylon cleaning pad. Do not use an abrasive scourer or steel wool.

---

Pyrolytic cleaning is a special process built in to some ovens. It requires you to set the empty oven to a very high temperature for a specified period of time. This turns the dirt to ashes which can be brushed out easily when the oven is cool.

---

If you are cooking something in the oven which may bubble over – like a fruit pie – use a baking tray to catch the spills. It will be easier to clean than the floor of the oven.

---

**Oven shelves** can be cleaned in the dishwasher or soaked in a solution of biological detergent – or in the bath (protecting the bath surface with old towels) if your sink is not big enough.

*Range cookers* Food tends to carbonise on the hot plates and in the hot ovens, so it can be simply brushed off with a wire brush. Spills should be wiped out of the cooler ovens with a damp cloth as soon as you have finished cooking. If the spill is left it can be difficult to remove; if this is the case, use a suitable cream cleaner (see 'Enamel', page 126).

To keep vitreous enamelled surfaces clean, wipe over regularly with a soapy damp cloth followed by a polish with a clean dry cloth. Mop up any spills containing acid (milk, fruit juice, etc.) immediately, as they can discolour the enamel.

Clean the insides of the hotplate lids and oven doors with a cream cleaner or a soap-impregnated pad, working in a circular motion. Do not immerse the oven doors in water as they contain insulation.

*Refrigerators*

Most modern fridges have an automatic defrosting device. If yours is an older model, switch off at the socket and defrost manually using the following method:

- Remove all food. Transfer perishable goods into a cool box containing freezer slabs.
- When defrosting is complete, remove the drip tray and empty out any water.

It is important not to damage the fridge while defrosting. The process can be speeded up by placing bowls of hot water on the shelves and renewing the water as it cools. You can also direct a hair-dryer or fan-heater on a low setting at the icy parts, taking care not to let any water near the appliance.

The fridge interior should be cleaned from time to time with a solution of bicarbonate of soda (15ml to 1 litre warm water), then dried well with a soft cloth. This is an odourless remedy, unlike soap or detergent solutions and some proprietary fridge-cleaning products. Wash shelves and other fitments in a hot solution of washing-up liquid. Rinse and dry well before replacing. Use an old towel to catch any drips.

If your fridge develops smells because of rotten food or because the power supply has been turned off, clear out all food and wash the interior several times with a bicarbonate of soda solution. Leave the fridge door open between washes until the smell has gone.

When you go away for any length of time (say, four weeks or more), empty the fridge of food and leave the door wedged slightly open with a tea-towel, so that air can circulate.

The exterior should be wiped over with a warm detergent solution. Dry and apply an aerosol cleaner/polish to keep dirt at bay.

Once or twice a year pull the fridge away from the wall and use a vacuum cleaner dusting attachment to remove dust from the grille on the back.

**Freezers**   *Defrosting* Unless your freezer is of the frost-free variety, it will need defrosting when the ice has grown to a thickness of approximately 5mm. The more often you open the door, the more often you will need to defrost. The method is as follows.

- Unplug the appliance.
- Put on gloves (special freezer gloves are available) to remove the frozen food and place it either in cool boxes or in the refrigerator. Cover with towels or blankets to increase insulation.
- Leave the freezer door open and place old towels on the freezer floor if it is a chest freezer or just in front of the freezer if it is an upright model.
- Place bowls of hot water on the shelves and in the bottom of the chest and keep renewing the water as it cools. (You can speed up drying with judicious use of a hair-dryer or fan-heater, but do not use the highest setting and do not put such appliances too near the freezer otherwise the seal may be damaged and the lining distorted.)
- Use a wooden or plastic spatula to loosen and scrape off the ice as thawing gets under way. As towels become saturated, replace them with new ones.

- When defrosting is finished, first dry the interior with a clean towel, then rinse with a solution of bicarbonate of soda (15ml soda to 1 litre water), then dry again.

After defrosting your freezer, paint a thin coating of glycerine over the interior to prevent frost building up, making it easier to clean the next time.

> Avoid ice building up in your freezer by keeping a log book of its contents and referring to that, rather than rifling through the contents to see what's in there, which increases fuel consumption.

*Smells* If smells linger, use a proprietary fridge/freezer cleaner or solution of sterilising fluid for babies' feeding bottles (one capful to 2 litres water) and allow to dry. Alternatively, fill the freezer with crumpled newspapers and leave it switched off with the door slightly ajar for a couple of days. The newspaper will absorb the smells. (You will need to call upon your neighbours or a friendly butcher to store your frozen food while this is going on.) Another, long-term, solution is to keep a container of cat litter in the freezer.

*Stains* These can be removed with neat bicarbonate of soda applied on a damp cloth.

To clean the freezer exterior, use a solution of washing-up liquid, then dry and spray with aerosol cleaner or polish.

### Microwaves

Wipe out the interior with a damp cloth if any spills occur. Keep the inside of the door and the seal scrupulously clean.

If smells build up, place a bowl of water containing 15ml lemon juice (bottled is fine) in the oven and run on high power for one minute. Remove the bowl and wipe round the oven cavity with a cloth, using the condensation which will have formed to clean it.

**Dishwashers**   Wipe the exterior with a mild detergent solution and apply aerosol cleaner or polish. The interior should be cleaned when smells build up by running an empty cycle with a proprietary dishwasher cleaner (see Chapter 9, Products that work)

**Extractor fans**   It is important that these are kept clean or they will not function properly. Follow the manufacturer's instructions for cleaning, if you have them; if not, use the following method.

- Switch off at the mains.
- Remove the flex socket from the main part of the fan and unscrew the front-louvred grille.
- Clean the grille in a solution of washing-up liquid. Allow to drain, then wipe with kitchen paper or a clean cloth to ensure it is thoroughly dry.
- To clean the fan blades, either use an anti-static brush or unscrew the blade unit and wash in soapy water. Use a teapot brush to reach into any crannies in the motor and its support.
- Re-assemble all parts of the fan and give it a trial run to ensure it is working properly.
- Replace the grille.

**Washing-machines and tumble-dryers**   The exterior should be wiped with a mild detergent solution followed by an application of aerosol cleaner/polish. Leave the washing-machine open for a while after removing a washload so that the interior can dry out and smells do not build up.

Remove the tumble-dryer filter after every session and clean off the fluff. Use a fluffy synthetic brush, which becomes static when stroked, or the crevice tool attachment of a vacuum cleaner. The hot air hose at the back should be cleaned regularly using the same method.

Washing-machines should be run on a clean-water-only cycle three or four times a year to clear any blockages.

Clean your washing-machine from time to time by running it with detergent but no load. In hard water areas add a little water softener to the detergent to get rid of any scale which may have built up.

## Cupboards

Kitchen cupboards should be cleaned out regularly several times a year. Remove the food from each cupboard before starting and throw away any items which are past their best. Wash out the interior with a mild detergent solution, then rinse with warm water and dry with kitchen paper or an old towel. Leave for a couple of hours or longer before replacing the food, to ensure that any residual dampness has gone.

There is no need to line the bases of cupboards unless they are made of bare untreated wood, in which case use a proprietary lining paper or a roll of wallpaper. Do *not* use ready-pasted paper as bugs enjoy the flavour of the paste.

## Wooden kitchen units

If untreated these will attract grease and dust, so wipe over regularly with a solution of washing-up liquid and apply a light coat of aerosol cleaner/polish. If dirt becomes a serious problem, clean the units thoroughly with a cream cleanser. Rinse, allow to dry and apply a coating of polyurethane seal. This will alter the appearance slightly but will make cleaning easier in future.

**Bins**  Kitchen bins should be emptied as soon as the contents start to smell, even if the bin liner is not full, and cleaned once a week with a solution of bleach or disinfectant (use the dilution strength recommended on the bottle). Always wear household gloves and protect your clothing from splashes. Drain the bin well after washing and if necessary wipe dry with kitchen paper. You will probably need to wash the bin top more often as it tends to attract dirt and splashes.

Always line kitchen bins before you put rubbish into them. Carrier bags are suitable for smaller bins, otherwise you will need to buy bin liners of the appropriate size. Some brands include a deodorising scent.

**Bakeware**  This includes cake tins, loaf tins, etc. and requires greater care than roasting tins. As a general rule the less you wash bakeware the better it performs. Ideally, just wipe with kitchen paper after use.

Always follow any special care instructions: some non-stick bakeware, for example, should be washed in clear water only, without washing-up liquid.

Burnt deposits can be loosened by soaking in a boiling solution of washing soda; do not try to scrape deposits off non-stick items with a knife.

Bakeware made from tin should be dried immediately after washing to prevent rusting.

**Bread bins**  These should be washed out, rinsed and dried once a week. If mould develops, wash and wipe the interior with neat white vinegar. Allow to dry before putting bread in.

**Chopping boards**  Chopping boards should be washed immediately after use.

***Wooden boards*** These should be washed under hot running water and scrubbed with a washing-up brush if necessary. Wipe over with a sterilising solution and stand the board on its long edge to dry naturally. Never soak a wooden board as this can cause warping. Where joints have opened up because of water seepage, lie the board flat and cover with a damp cloth for a few hours to make the wood swell. Wipe over with a little vegetable oil when dry. Always store the board on its side so that air can reach both surfaces. Smells can be removed by rubbing with half a lemon dipped in salt.

***Plastic boards*** These can usually be washed in the dishwasher. If not, wash as for wooden boards.

### Cutlery

See 'Tableware', page 67.

### Food processors

Wash the plastic parts by hand using a solution of washing-up liquid. Those that can go in dishwashers should be put on the top rack, where the temperature is lower. Metal parts can usually be washed in a dishwasher, but check the instruction booklet. Keep the parts with electrical connections out of the water, and use a damp cloth to wipe over the surrounding areas.

### Glassware

See 'Tableware', page 67.

### Ironing boards

On the whole these do not need cleaning since they come into contact only with clean items. Use a general-purpose lubricant spray to keep the moving parts flexible and launder fabric covers occasionally. Put them back on when damp, as they may shrink, and then iron dry. Bear in mind that metallised fabric covers are more effective than cotton ones at retaining heat and speeding up the ironing process.

*Irons*    Always follow the manufacturer's instructions for cleaning both the inside and the base of your iron. Some steam irons need regular descaling, particularly in hard water areas. Use the descaling product recommended by the manufacturer. Some irons incorporate a built-in cartridge, which should be changed when colour alteration shows a build-up of scale.

Where scorching has occurred on the base, use very fine steel wool to remove the marks, taking care not to scratch the surface. Starch marks can be removed by rubbing the base of the iron with soap while still warm.

*Kettles*    Kettles build up furry deposits, especially in hard water areas. Proprietary descaler products are available to treat this problem; always follow the instructions carefully. It is best to descale a kettle before the fur has formed a thick layer or you may have to repeat the treatment several times. Always wear protective gloves. The exterior should be wiped regularly.

*Knives*    **Wooden-handled** knives must be washed by hand. **Carbon-steel-blade** knives should be washed and dried immediately after use, otherwise they will rust. They also tend to discolour when they come into contact with certain foods; stains can be removed with a nylon pad or abrasive cleaning powder.

Knife handles made from a suitable material such as plastic are dishwashable, but if the handle and blade are made separately and glued together with a tang (a sharp prong projecting from the blade) fixed in the handle, the knives are better washed by hand and dried immediately so that hot water cannot penetrate the join and loosen the adhesive.

Knife handles made from **bone, ceramic, horn, ivory, mother-of-pearl** and so on (see also pages 129–31) should be kept out of water and just polished with a soft cloth. You do not put them in your mouth so this is not unhygienic. If you are unable to wash knives with mother-of-pearl handles soon after use, soak the knife blades taking care to keep the handles out of the water.

*Plastics*

Plastic items are generally safe in dishwashers if they are rigid; if flexible they are likely to melt and should be washed by hand. If stains build up on plastic tableware they can be removed with a very weak solution of bleach or denture cleaning powder.

Smelly plastic containers should be filled with a bicarbonate of soda solution (45ml to 500ml water) and left overnight before rinsing.

*Roasting tins*

Fill the tin with water and half a handful of washing soda. Boil for a few minutes, rinse and dry.

> If you wash the roasting tin and replace it in the oven while the oven is still warm, the residual heat will dry it out.

*Saucepans*

Saucepans come in a wide variety of materials and finishes, some of which require special care. If you buy a pan with an unusual finish, remember to keep the instructions; some of the more delicate finishes can be damaged by cleaning with the wrong product. Never put saucepans with wooden handles in the dishwasher unless the manufacturer states that the wood will be safe. Note, too, that some plastic handles may melt in the dishwasher, particularly if the pan is placed on the lower rack near the heating element.

To shift burnt-on deposits, fill the pan with a solution of biological detergent such as Biotex and leave for a couple of hours. Change the solution as soon as it turns brown; after soaking bring it to the boil and remove as much deposit as possible. Severe stains may require several treatments.

*Aluminium pans* should be washed as soon as possible after use since food and water can cause the surface to pit. Wash either in the dishwasher or by hand and dry immediately. Use a scouring pad or steel wool soap pad to shine up the surface. If the interior has become discoloured, boil up a weak acid solution of apple peel or lemon juice in water. Rinse and dry. Do not use bleach.

*Cast-iron pans* should be washed immediately after use and dried at once, otherwise rust may develop. If it does, use a wire wool soap pad.

---

To remove food smells from any pan, boil a panful of water containing 30ml white vinegar. Switch on your extractor fan if you have one so that the smell of vinegar does not permeate the whole house.

---

*Copper pans* are usually lined with tin as the acids in certain foods react adversely with copper. Wash by hand, using a copper cleaner or salt and white vinegar to keep the exterior clean and shiny. Note that the lining of copper pans eventually wears thin and the pan will need to be recoated.

*Non-stick pans* should be cleaned according to the care instructions. Some are dishwasher-safe, others just need wiping out with kitchen paper.

Note that even where the use of metal implements to remove burnt deposits is permitted, jabbing hard with them will damage the finish.

If washing non-stick ware by hand, take care not to use anything abrasive on the surface. A nylon pad should remove any grease deposits. If staining occurs, soak the pan in a solution of one cup of water, half a cup of household bleach and 30g bicarbonate of soda. Boil this mixture for a few minutes, then wash, rinse and dry the pan.

***Stainless steel pans*** can be washed by hand or in the dishwasher. Use a stainless steel cleaner to remove stains on the outside of the pan. The base may be aluminium or copper as these materials conduct heat better. Aluminium should be washed and copper cleaned with a copper cleaner. Do not soak stainless steel pans for long or pitting from mineral salts in the water may occur.

***Vitreous enamel pans*** can be washed by hand or in the dishwasher. Stains on the outside of the pan should be removed with a suitable product (see 'Enamel', page 126). If the inside of the pan becomes stained, soak it in water with 5ml bleach for a few hours, then wash as normal.

> A milk pan will be easier to clean if you rinse it out with cold water before heating the milk.

### Sieves

Clean immediately after use, before the sieved residue has a chance to harden and dry. Hold the sieve upside down under running water and use a washing-up or bottle brush to ensure that all the débris is removed from the holes.

### Tableware

Received wisdom about the order for washing-up by hand is: glass, cutlery, then crockery – this way you start with the least dirty and work up to the most dirty. It makes sense as long as you dry up as you go along.

Two sinks make the task easier; if you only have one, use a large plastic bowl for rinsing to speed up the process.

> Never wash in a dishwasher very fine china, china with a hand-painted surface which is not safely glazed or china with a silver or gold trim.

***Cutlery*** (See also 'Knives', page 64.) This should be washed as soon as possible after a meal, especially if made of bronze or silver (see pages 125 and 127), which stain easily. Do not immerse bone or mother-of-pearl handles in water and *never* wash them in a dishwasher. Soak the blades in water, keeping the handles clean.

Silver cutlery which is not used regularly should be wrapped in tarnish-proof cutlery rolls or paper. See 'Silver and silver plate', page 127.

> Do not wash silver and stainless steel cutlery together in a dishwasher: an electrolytic reaction could cause particles of silver to transfer on to the stainless steel.

> Black boiled-egg stains on silver spoons can be removed by rubbing with a damp cloth dipped in salt. Rinse immediately afterwards. Ideally, eat boiled eggs with stainless-steel spoons.

***Glasses and glassware*** Valuable glassware pieces should be washed individually and dried while still warm. Take care not to knock them on taps, and wear well-fitting household gloves to reduce the chance of dropping them. See 'Drinking glasses', page 121.

*Plates and casserole dishes* Whether using a dishwasher or washing by hand, first rinse off all food in warm water, or run the pre-wash program once you have stacked the plates in the machine. However, if the food residue is starchy or tenacious (e.g. mashed potato, egg or milk), rinse in cold water as warm water will make the residue more difficult to remove.

Greasy plates are easier to clean if first soaked in warm water with a little washing soda.

---

**Fishy smells**
- If fishy smells linger on plates, add a little vinegar to the final rinse water; cutlery should be rubbed with lemon juice and rinsed immediately.
- When your hands become smelly from handling fish, do not wash them immediately as this tends to set the smell. Rub them first with lemon juice. Other useful products include Wonder Bar and Fresh Hands – a steel 'egg' you wipe your hands on (see Chapter 9, Products that work).

---

## Teapots

Teapots tend to build up tannin stains with use. Some people prefer not to wash them with detergent or in a dishwasher as they claim this taints the tea flavour. If you find this to be the case, be sure to rinse out the pot with water immediately after use.

*China teapots* Clean the inside by soaking in a solution of denture cleaner or a product designed to clean plastic tableware or picnicware. Rinse thoroughly after cleaning and leave off the lid so that any residual smell dissipates quickly.

***Silver and stainless steel teapots*** Rinse after use and wash in a solution of washing-up liquid from time to time. The value of a silver teapot may be reduced if you use a strong chemical cleaner to get rid of tannin stains. Instead, rub with either a handful of clean milk bottle tops or aluminium foil, dipped in a solution of washing soda and boiling water. Leave for a few minutes, rinse and dry.

> To prevent smells from building up in a silver or stainless steel teapot, leave three or four sugar lumps wrapped in muslin in the pot between uses. Make sure the teapot has been dried thoroughly before replacing the sugar lumps.

***Toasters*** These just need wiping over. The instructions should tell you how to remove crumbs from the inside. Never try to dislodge burnt particles with a sharp implement, even when the toaster is switched off at the socket.

***Vegetable racks*** Use the bath to wash these in a solution of washing-up liquid – line the bath with old towels to protect its surface. Use a scourer to get rid of ingrained dirt and rinse in clean water. Plastic and plastic-coated racks should be left to drain; metal racks should be dried immediately with an old towel.

***Vacuum flasks*** These should be washed out as soon as possible after use. If the smell of the liquid lingers, fill the flask with hot water and 15ml bicarbonate of soda. Do not immerse in water as the flask will be damaged. Store with the top off and a couple of sugar lumps inside to keep it fresh.

An electrical waste disposal unit is particularly useful if you live in an upstairs flat or anywhere that poses problems with disposing of rubbish. Keep the unit clean, do not drop teaspoons down it and get rid of any smells by grinding up waste citrus peel from grapefruit, lemons and oranges.

*Waste disposal units*

Wood should be washed and dried immediately after use; do not soak, otherwise the wood may warp. Items which collect food débris, such as chopping boards (see page 62), cheese and pastry boards and pastry rollers, should be scraped gently first with a blunt knife.

*Wooden items*

***Wooden salad bowls*** should be wiped out with kitchen paper or a cloth wrung out in clean warm water and left to dry naturally. They should not be washed. From time to time, season the outside of the bowl with a little vegetable oil and rub in well.

## The bathroom

While you are unlikely to come to any harm if you do not clean the living and sleeping areas of your home very often, failure to clean the bathroom, as with the kitchen, could prove to be a health hazard. It takes only a few minutes a day to keep the bathroom clean.

---

**Daily cleaning**
- Keep a bottle of washing-up liquid or bathroom cleaner and a cellulose sponge in the bathroom and encourage everyone to wipe round the bath and washbasin after use. This prevents hard water deposits and soap splashes building up.
- The lavatory should be checked daily and any dirt sticking to the bowl should be removed with a lavatory brush then flushed away. Once or twice a week, depending on the dirt level, clean more thoroughly.

---

**Basins and bidets** These are usually vitreous- or porcelain-enamelled and should be cleaned in the same way as baths (see below).

**Baths** These should be cleaned according to what they are made from. Keep and follow any manufacturers' instructions if you have a newly installed bath, or send off for a new set if you buy a home with a bath made from unfamiliar material.

*Acrylic baths* These should be rinsed and dried with a soft cloth after use, especially when additives such as bubble bath have been used, as these leave deposits on the surface. Clean with washing-up liquid. Where hard water deposits have built up, use a cream cleaner, rinse and buff.

Where the surface is scratched, rub gently with a cream metal cleaner or polish and buff well when the mark has gone. Bear in mind that metal cleaner removes some of the top layer so try to avoid scratching the bath. Deep scratches can be eradicated by rubbing gently with very fine wet-and-dry paper (used wet). Rub with metal cleaner, rinse and buff.

*Glass-fibre baths* These need particular care as their colour is in the surface coating only; if rubbed with abrasives or metal polish the colour will eventually disappear. Clean regularly with washing-up liquid and avoid allowing deposits to build up or scratches to occur.

*Vitreous- and porcelain-enamelled baths* These should be cleaned only with a product suitable for enamel (see 'Enamel', page 126). Do not use harsh abrasives as they will eventually dull the bath's surface. Stubborn marks should respond to rubbing with paraffin, turpentine or white spirit. Rinse with a hot solution of washing-up liquid, then wipe dry.

Blue-green marks on enamel baths are the result of a constantly dripping tap. The washer should be changed and a vitreous enamel cleaner used, repeating several times if necessary.

---

**Bathroom mirrors and windows**
- If you run cold water into the bath before hot, the bathroom windows and mirrors will not steam up so badly.
- Rub bathroom mirrors with a little neat washing-up liquid to prevent condensation. (See also 'Mirrors', page 121.)

---

Tide marks should be treated with vitreous enamel cleaner. If the stain is very heavy, rub with white spirit, then rinse off immediately with a solution of washing-up liquid. Repeat if necessary until the mark clears but *do not* leave the white spirit to work on its own.

Use a proprietary bath stain remover for rust stains. Hard water marks should respond to a vitreous enamel cleaner; otherwise use a sanitaryware cleaner that incorporates a scale remover.

***Bath sealant*** which develops mouldy areas should be cleaned with household bleach applied on an old toothbrush. Take care not to get bleach on surrounding areas, towels or your

---

Do not leave your houseplants in the bath whilst on holiday as chemicals from the soil can cause permanent staining. Stand them in washing-up bowls or plastic or glass mixing bowls, out of sight of passers-by who could infer that you are away. Ideally, don't stand them in water but have a separate bowl of water nearby with a piece of towelling 'wicking' leading from the bowl to underneath the plant pot. Even better, ask neighbours to do plant duty!

---

clothes. Rinse thoroughly, then use a fungicidal wash to delay recurrence.

---

**Cleaning chrome**

To remove scale from the chrome areas of a bath or basin – the plughole, taps and soak-away – rub with half a lemon or with vinegar, then rinse off and dry with a paper towel.

---

**Showers**

*Shower cubicle* Wipe after use, including the curtain or doors. Leave the curtain slightly open so that air can circulate.

*Shower curtains* If these develop mildew, first soak them in a bleach solution (one part to four parts water), then rinse and machine-wash. Mildew-resistant shower curtains are available. (See also 'Mildew', page 37.) Hard water deposits on shower walls should be wiped over with neat white vinegar. Leave on for 15 minutes, then rinse with the shower-head. Slimy shower curtains should be soaked in warm water to which a little fabric conditioner has been added. Rinse and wipe dry.

*Shower-head* If this is clogged, take it apart and soak the pieces (apart from the rubber washer) in neat white malt vinegar. Use an old toothbrush to remove sediment before putting the shower-head together again. Proprietary shower-head cleaners are also available.

**Lavatories**

Daily brushing and flushing and a once-a-week clean with a special lavatory cleaner should be sufficient for the lavatory bowl. Bleach is not generally recommended as it damages the ceramic glaze and makes the lavatory more difficult to clean; if you do use it, do not leave it for more than five minutes before flushing.

Where stains and hard water deposits have formed deep inside the bowl, you will first need to remove the water. The easiest way to do this is to bale it out using a disposable cup. Then apply thick, undiluted bleach to the stain and rinse off immediately; re-apply at intervals until the stain has gone. Hard water deposits should be covered with a thick paste of laundry borax and vinegar; leave for a couple of hours, then brush off and rinse. Ring marks can be removed with a proprietary limescale remover.

Always flush a lavatory free of chemicals before using it. The splashing could damage your skin.

> Never mix different brands of lavatory cleaner, or lavatory cleaner and bleach, in the bowl at the same time. A chemical reaction may give off toxic fumes.

*Lavatory brush* Wash regularly in hot soapy water and rinse in cold water with a few drops of disinfectant to stiffen the bristles. Wash the holder as well, if you have one.

*Lavatory seat* Wipe on top and underneath once a day using a solution of warm water with a little disinfectant. Dry with kitchen paper. Keep a cloth specifically for this purpose and do not use it for anything else.

*Lavatory pedestal* Wash the outside once a week.

## Taps

*Chromium taps* just need a wipe with a damp cloth. Buff dry. Greasy marks should come off with washing-up liquid; for more serious stains use a liquid-metal cleaner or some metal-cleaning wadding – but nothing abrasive.

If the mouth of a tap is encrusted with limescale, cut down a yoghurt pot to about an inch high, fill it with white malt vinegar or a proprietary limescale remover, then suspend it from the tap head with masking tape so that the spout is immersed in the liquid. Check after an hour or so to see whether the scale has gone and repeat if necessary. Wash and polish the tap.

**Gold-plated taps** need to be dried with a soft cloth after use, otherwise marks will appear. Do not use a proprietary cleaner as this will eventually wear away the surface.

**Ceramic tiles** Where soap splashes have built up, wipe over with a white vinegar solution (one part vinegar to four parts water), then rinse and wipe dry. Using a spray cleaner with a mould inhibitor is effective.

Dirty grouting should be cleaned with a bleach solution (one part bleach to six parts water) applied on an old toothbrush. Make sure the floor is protected from splashes. A proprietary grout cleaner can also be used.

**Plugholes and overflows** Accumulated gunge should be cleaned out of these once a week, using a bottle brush or teapot brush. Pour down a little liquid bleach, leave for a couple of minutes, then rinse with clear water; this will also help to eliminate smells.

**Rubber plugs** These should be cleaned with turpentine.

**Shower and bath mats** **Rubber** These tend to collect dirt in their indentations and the only way to clean them is a good scrub with washing-up liquid and a brush. Rinse thoroughly so that slime does not develop, and clean the mats on a regular basis.

**Candlewick bath mats** Launder or dry-clean according to the care label. Never tumble-dry as this will melt the foam backing.

If these become slimy, soak them in a white vinegar solution (15ml vinegar to 500ml water) – or one to which you have added a little lemon juice – for at least two hours, then wash well.

*Sponges and flannels*

Natural sponges, which can be hard and gritty when new, should be soaked in cold water until soft, squeezed out and then covered in boiling water for five minutes.

## Beds and bedding

Beds and bedding will last longer, and you will sleep better, if they are aired each day after use. The human body loses about 300ml of moisture a night, and at least 20 minutes of thorough airing are needed for it to evaporate from a mattress and bedding, so encourage all members of your household to throw back their bedclothes when they get up. Always make beds *before* you start cleaning a room, as dust is inevitably generated.

These should be washed according to the care label. Dark-dyed colours should be washed separately from other colours until you are sure that the item is colour-fast.

*Duvet covers, pillow cases and sheets*

*Mixed-fibre sheets, etc.* should not need ironing provided you fold them as soon as they are dry.
*Natural-fibre bedding* looks better if it is ironed; this will be easier if you fold the item into four and attach it with three pegs to a clothes line. Iron when still slightly damp and air thoroughly before replacing on the bed.

After washing white cotton or linen sheets always place them at the bottom of the pile in the linen cupboard. Regular rotation and use prevents yellow marks developing on the folds. Do not store white cotton or linen bedding in an airing cupboard or yellowing might occur.

> Duvet covers, pillow cases and sheets will dry more quickly if pegged to form a 'bag'. To achieve this effect with a sheet, fold it once along its length and peg the two pairs of ends to the line. Peg a third of the way along one side and a third of the way along the other side. With duvet covers and pillow cases peg one side only so that a good-sized opening is left for air to get into.

**Pillows**  Pillows are either foam-filled or made from synthetic or natural fibres. Avoid natural fillings if you are asthmatic or allergic to feathers and down. Bear in mind that some foam tends to become lumpy with use.

Pillows should be plumped up every day and both natural and synthetic-fibre pillows will benefit from an airing on a clothes line in fine, breezy weather.

As a general rule, pillows should be washed only when it is essential; even careful washing does not improve their texture. However, always read the care label as some are unaffected by washing. People with dust allergies should have their pillows cleaned regularly, either by hand-washing – in which case allow plenty of time for natural drying and airing – or in a machine. Bear in mind that a pillow becomes heavy when wet and may be too much for a domestic machine; if this is the case, go to a launderette and use a centrifugal dryer to remove as much moisture as possible.

Never dry-clean pillows as it is impossible to ensure that all toxic fumes have been removed from the filling.

Pillows can be hand-washed in the bath using a solution of soapflakes or a mild detergent, using the following method.

- Knead the pillow quite vigorously in the suds so that all the filling is soaked.
- Rinse several times in clear warm water.
- Wring out as much water as possible by letting the water out of the bath and pressing down hard on the pillow.
- Roll the pillow in an old towel to stop it dripping on the floor.
- If you have a spin-dryer, spin the pillow for a maximum of 30 seconds (any longer and the filling could be damaged). Otherwise leave it to dry naturally, either pegged to a clothes line or spread on a special stretcher designed for drying jumpers flat. Do not tumble-dry.
- Air thoroughly before putting the pillow back on the bed.

Pillows will stay in better condition if you use two pillow cases. The double thickness prevents hair gel, face cream, etc. from seeping into the filling. Use an old pillow case for the inner layer.

For care of pillow cases, see 'Duvet covers, pillow cases and sheets', page 77.

> You can tell when a pillow is past its best by placing it width-ways over your forearm. If it holds its shape it's fine; if it droops badly at either end, you should invest in a new one.

## Duvets

Like pillows, duvets need regular and thorough airing, preferably in the open air. If this is not possible, drape the duvet over the bottom of a bedstead or a couple of chairbacks. A duvet cover should always be used to protect the duvet from body moisture and spills.

Treat spills on the duvet immediately by tying off the affected area tightly with string, having first shaken the filling away from the

outer casing. Clean according to the stain and the fabric.

This method can also be used when you want to wash the whole duvet casing. Shake the filling down to one end and tie the string tightly round the middle. Wash half the duvet casing and allow to dry, then shake the filling to the other end and repeat the process.

Do not attempt to wash any duvet (even a single) in a domestic washing-machine. Duvets are so bulky when wet that they can damage the spin cycle. Go to a launderette or have the duvet cleaned professionally. For a list of cleaners in your area contact the Textile Services Association (see 'Textiles' in Addresses section).

---

**Putting on a clean duvet cover**

Putting on a clean duvet cover, especially a double or king-size one, can be tricky and frustrating. It is easier with two people, but if you are alone turn the duvet cover inside-out and push your arms through the opening into the far corners. With one hand in each corner, grasp the two corresponding corners of the duvet through the cover and shake down vigorously so that the cover envelops the duvet; it will now be right-side-out.

---

**Eiderdowns**  These should be dry-cleaned professionally and aired thoroughly before use to ensure no toxic fumes remain.

**Blankets**  Blankets may be made of natural or synthetic fibres or a mixture of the two. They benefit from a spell out of use as this reduces pilling – so if possible rotate your supply, storing those not in use in sealed plastic bags or special blanket bags (available from most department stores). Wash them before storing and put a moth-repellent sachet in with those containing any wool.

You can wash a blanket in a domestic washing-machine provided that it can hold it comfortably when dry. If the blanket is too big, wash by hand in the bath or take it to a launderette.

Follow the steps below when hand-washing a blanket.

- An initial soak in clean cold bath water will remove surface dirt, but if the blanket is heavily stained soak first in biological detergent, taking care to immerse the *entire* blanket in case of colour change.
- Wash in a solution of mild detergent (easier to rinse out than soapflakes), kneading with your hands so that all areas are agitated.
- Rinse several times in warm clear water, putting 30ml olive oil in the final rinse to soften the blanket.
- Empty the bath and wring out as much water as possible, pressing down hard with your hands. Do not twist the blanket (a tempting option when there are two people), as this can damage the fibres.
- Put the blanket in a spin-dryer if you have one, and tumble-dry if the care label permits. Otherwise let it dry naturally, preferably outdoors. (Note that the blanket will dry more quickly if you ensure that the two wet sides are not in contact with each other.)
- Always hang striped blankets with the colours running vertically so that colours stay in their intended lines.
- Air the blanket thoroughly before storing or use.

***Electric blankets*** There are various kinds of electric blanket, from pre-heating underblankets which you switch on before you go to bed and then turn off, to low-voltage, all-night under- or overblankets. Electric duvets are also available. Always follow the manufacturer's care instructions for your own blanket. Many types can be washed but this should be done as infrequently as possible; fortunately regular washing is unlikely to be necessary.

Most manufacturers recommend that electric blankets are returned to them for servicing every two or three years, at which point they will advise you whether the blanket needs replacing and may offer a price reduction on a new model.

Do not fold electric blankets when storing them: this may damage the element. Ideally, leave them flat on a spare bed or between a mattress and a bed base.

**Sheepskin and wool underblankets** are washable. Use plenty of fabric conditioner when machine-washing; when hand-washing put a teaspoon of olive oil in the final rinse to keep the fabric soft and supple.

**Bedspreads (counterpanes)** These should be laundered or dry-cleaned according to the care label. Always air thoroughly after dry-cleaning to make sure that all the fumes have dissipated. (Specialist bedding cleaners should do this for you, but always check.) Do not use a coin-operated machine to clean bedding, because the fumes will linger within it unless you give it hours of outdoor airing.

**Candlewick bedspreads** should be dried on a clothes line with the fluffy side on the inside. To make the pile stand up, rub the insides together or tumble-dry.

**Mattresses** These stay in better condition for longer if a protective cover is put over the mattress casing. The cover should be washed at regular intervals according to the fabric.

Mattresses should be turned over as often as the manufacturer recommends (this is much easier if two people tackle the job) or, if no recommendation is given, monthly or more often when new and then at six-monthly intervals. Every three months the head and foot of the mattress should be reversed. **Foam mattresses** do not need to be turned since they do not absorb the shape of bodies in the same way as sprung mattresses, but should still be reversed every three months. A **double mattress** should be turned more frequently if the two people who sleep on it are of very different weights.

Dust can be removed from a **sprung mattress** with a soft brush; if your vacuum cleaner has a soft-brush attachment, set it on a low suction level. It is important not to pull out the buttons or to disturb the filling. **Foam mattresses** should be vacuumed with a crevice tool attachment set on a low suction level.

Make sure that the bed is pulled out at least once a week and the floor underneath it vacuumed to collect any skin-scale or dust which has accumulated. (See pages 27 and 46 for information on getting blood and urine stains out of mattresses.)

*Bed bases*

These should be vacuumed, using the appropriate tool for the material – a soft dusting brush for upholstery; a crevice tool for wooden slats. Make sure that the castors run smoothly; use a little oil or aerosol lubricator if they seem stiff, taking care to protect the flooring.

*Futons*

These are designed to be rolled up loosely each day so that air can circulate through them and the moisture dry out. Follow the manufacturer's instructions.

## Carpets and rugs

New carpets should come supplied with care instructions. Keep these in a safe place and follow them carefully to ensure you get maximum wear out of the carpets. Some new carpets come with a protective coating such as Scotchgard. This can also be applied after fitting and should always be re-applied after shampooing.

*Vacuuming*

The best way to keep carpets clean is to vacuum regularly – at least once a week and more often in areas where there is heavy wear. (See page 14 for more about vacuum cleaners.)

- Always make sure your vacuum cleaner is set to the correct level of suction for the carpet you want to clean.
- Purists say you should go over each piece of carpet about eight times in order to be sure that it is thoroughly clean – but most people are satisfied with the results produced by a couple of forward and backward movements.
- Use any special attachments provided to reach under heavy pieces of furniture that cannot be moved and to clean around the edges of a room where dirt tends to accumulate.
- Some years ago it was received wisdom that you should not vacuum a new carpet until it had been laid down for several weeks. Manufacturers now encourage vacuuming as soon as a carpet is laid, and although you may find at first that it sheds fluff at what appears to be an alarming rate, rest assured that removing the fluff does not harm the carpet.
- Some things, such as dressmaking threads, pine needles and pet hairs, are difficult to vacuum up. Using an attachment may solve the problem; otherwise you may have to pick them off by hand. Pet hairs can be collected on a damp sponge or sticky tape (masking tape or Sellotape).

> Do not re-use vacuum cleaner bags unless the manufacturer says you can. With repeated use they become porous and do not trap the dust properly.

*Long-pile (shag) carpets and loop-pile carpets* should be cleaned with a suction-only vacuum cleaner; the rotating brush of an upright cleaner can abrade long-pile carpets or catch in loop-pile carpets. If you go over the pile before vacuuming with a carpet rake (available from carpet retailers, but do not use on loop-pile carpet) you will loosen any tangles and some embedded dirt. You should also rake the carpet after vacuuming if you want all the pile to lie in the same direction.

> When vacuuming fringed rugs, use a vacuum cleaner attachment with an old stocking over the nozzle to prevent the fringe from being sucked up into the appliance.

> Where furniture has made a dent in a carpet, melt an ice-cube in the dent and raise the pile with a brush when dry.

## Shampooing

When a carpet becomes heavily soiled it will need to be shampooed. You can do this at home with a domestic or hired machine, or call in a professional company to do it for you. However, don't shampoo carpets more often than is strictly necessary. Each shampoo takes a bit of life out of the carpet.

In general, **fitted carpets** are best cleaned in position since taking them up and sending them off to be cleaned may not only be expensive but can result in shrinkage.

It is best to seek professional help if you need to clean a large area of carpet, as it is a time-consuming and tiring job. (See page 19 for advice on employing cleaning contractors. The National Carpet Cleaners' Association (see 'Carpets' in Addresses section) will supply a list of its members. Professionals use machines that extract dirt from the bottom of the pile without over-wetting the carpet – important if the carpet is to keep its shape.

If you are doing the job yourself, take care not to over-wet the carpet; this may distort the backing and cause colour from the backing to . come through to the surface of the carpet.

---

**Protecting your carpet**

Whether you clean your carpets yourself or employ a professional firm, you should ensure that small pieces of aluminium foil are put under any furniture legs that are in contact with the cleaned carpet (reliable firms will do this automatically). This is to prevent the furniture from staining the wet carpet. The foil should be left in position until the carpet is thoroughly dry (which may take a day or so). It is easier for whoever is cleaning the carpet if as much furniture as possible is removed from the room before cleaning starts.

---

Before shampooing, brush the carpet with a stiff brush to loosen embedded dirt, then vacuum thoroughly, going over each area several times.

**Lightly soiled carpets** can then be cleaned by using an absorbent cloth and a bucket of water. Do not use a detergent as it may leave a sticky residue which speeds up the rate of re-soiling; there is also a risk of colour change due to bleach and brighteners.

**Heavily soiled carpets** will need a full shampoo. If a carpet is fitted, check that it is firmly secured or it may become loose and lose its shape as you shampoo. Use a special carpet shampoo, following any recommendations made by the manufacturer of the machine you are using. Do not make the shampoo solution any stronger than is recommended, even if your carpet is filthy.

Work over the carpet in sections, blotting each section as you go with an old white towel, then brush the pile into the right direction with a clean carpet brush and allow to dry thoroughly. Repeat the whole process after a few days. (See Chapter 2, Stain removal, for specific treatments.)

---

Nylon carpets create static and you may find you get slight shocks from metal items such as light switches and door fittings. If this becomes a problem, fill a plant spray container with water and 15ml fabric softener and spray on the carpet. Alternatively, you could call in a specialist firm to apply an anti-static coating. (Most carpet-fitting firms will do this with Scotchgard or a similar product. Do not attempt it yourself or the effect could be patchy.) This will need to be re-applied every time you shampoo the carpet.

---

## Steam cleaning

Steam cleaning is an excellent method of getting dirt out of your carpets. A steam-cleaning machine works by injecting a blast of steam into the carpet and then sucking it back so that the dirt comes out with it. One great advantage is that the carpet does not become too wet. You can either hire a machine or call in a professional to do the job for you. It is worth noting that the machines are quite tiring to use; if you are not particularly fit or strong, professional help is recommended. (See page 19 for advice on this.) Ensure that you protect carpet under furniture legs (see box on page 86).

**Foam-backed carpets**

Be careful when shampooing foam-backed carpets not to get the backing wet, as this can distort the carpet. Either use a steam-cleaning machine or a dry shampoo. Foam-backed carpets should never be used where there is under-floor heating.

**Oriental carpets**

Oriental carpets should be treated with care; they are hand-made and the materials used may have different degrees of colour fastness. Vacuum with a cylinder vacuum cleaner (an upright will drag the fibres) and avoid the fringes, which can get sucked up into the appliance – alternatively, cover the nozzle with an old stocking. Always vacuum in the direction in which the pile is intended to lie.

If a carpet is marked with grease, use a dry spot cleaner, testing first on an inconspicuous part of the carpet (e.g. the edge).

If applying any water-based treatment, sponge carefully and never allow water to penetrate to the back of the rug. Over-wetting of any kind can cause wool to distort.

If valuable, always use the services of an expert to clean your carpet (see 'Carpets' in Addresses section).

---

Test dye fastness by dampening a small area to see whether loose dye comes off on to a white tissue. If it does, have the carpet cleaned by an expert.

---

Most rugs can be vacuumed and shampooed in the same way as carpets (see above). The manufacturer's label should give cleaning instructions.

*Rugs*

---

Use an old tennis racquet to beat rugs. Hang the rug over a clothes line and give it a good whacking to remove dust.

---

*Oriental rugs* Do not shampoo **Chinese** or **Persian** rugs yourself but consult an expert (see 'Oriental carpets', opposite). Some **Indian** and **Turkish** rugs are woven without pile and can be shampooed.

*Sheepskin rugs* should be washed by hand using the following method.

- Boil 1 litre water, 175g soapflakes and 50ml olive oil together in a pan, stirring well so that the mixture emulsifies.
- Put the rug and mixture in a bath or large sink and add 50ml glycerine and enough warm water to cover the sheepskin.
- Wash well, making sure that all parts of the fleece are thoroughly agitated.
- Rinse once in deep warm water. Not all the soap will come out but some residue is important for retaining suppleness.
- Squeeze the rug to remove surplus water, then rub both sides of the sheepskin with a clean white towel.
- Hang the rug on a line in the open air until almost dry.
- Mix 125g fine oatmeal with 125g flour and rub the mixture into the underside of the rug; this replaces lost tanning materials and helps to keep it soft.
- When the rug is completely dry, brush the wool to separate the strands.

*Goatskin rugs* should be cleaned professionally as goat hair is brittle and tends to break off if washed.

*Rag rugs* should be hand-washed in warm water with soapflakes. Pull carefully into shape after washing and dry flat. Do not use artificial heat when drying.

## Floors

Floors should be cleaned regularly, since they are the most used surface in the home. Placing mats both outside and inside external doors will help to keep walked in débris to a minimum.

*Ceramic tiles*   These are easily cleaned with a mop or cloth dipped in a solution of washing-up liquid. Alternatively, clean with neat laundry borax applied on a damp mop or a solution of one part ammonia to three parts hot water. A squeegee mop is best for this type of floor as it removes most of the water. Be careful when walking on wet ceramic tiles as they are very slippery. Polish with a chamois leather. Do not use polish on the tiles as this will make them permanently slippery.

Grouting between the tiles should be cleaned from time to time with an old toothbrush dipped into a strong solution of washing-up liquid or household cleaner. Alternatively, use a special grout cleaner.

*Concrete*   Concrete floors just need regular sweeping. To keep dust to a minimum apply two coats of a PVA adhesive and water mixture (one part adhesive to five parts water), allowing the first coat to dry before applying the second.

*Cork tiles*   These usually have a sealed, waxed or vinyl finish to prevent water and dirt from penetrating their porous surface. (If you are laying cork tiles check that the edges as well as the surfaces are sealed or water may seep in from the sides.)

**Sealed cork** just needs mopping over with warm water. Emulsion polish should be applied occasionally.

**Vinyl-finished** cork should be damp-mopped, and emulsion polish applied occasionally.

**Waxed cork** should be swept regularly and wax or liquid polish applied occasionally.

When applying any of these polishes, try to avoid a build-up of polish around the edges of the room; this will eventually form a sticky deposit that attracts dirt and in bathrooms, substances such as talcum powder. It looks very unattractive and is difficult to remove (use the back of a knife blade).

---

Always rinse floor mops in a disinfectant solution after use. Hang off the ground or upside-down to dry.

---

*Linoleum*

Linoleum is very tough but should never be over-wetted. Use a mop dampened in a weak solution of household cleaner, then (when dry) apply a wax polish on living-room surfaces and an emulsion polish (which will not watermark) on kitchen and bathroom surfaces.

*Natural floorcoverings*

These include **cane, coconut matting, rush** and **sisal**, among other materials, and should be vacuumed regularly. When soiled, scrub first with salted and then clear water; these floor coverings are damaged by detergents. Some specialist companies can supply natural flooring with a protective finish, applied before fitting, which keeps dirt at bay.

**Parquet**  See 'Wood', opposite.

**Quarry tiles**  *Glazed tiles* should be washed with a weak solution of household cleaner. They should be polished with a liquid or paste wax polish, preferably a non-slip product.

*Unglazed tiles* will need a more vigorous scrub with a stronger solution.

Always rinse with warm clear water and wipe over with a dry mop.

*Faded tiles* can be restored to their original colour. Remove the polish by rubbing with steel wool and white spirit, then wash with household cleaner, rinse and allow to dry. Apply a thin coat of coloured wax polish and rub it in well so that it doesn't come off on the soles of your shoes.

*Newly laid tiles* tend to develop white patches, caused by lime working its way up through the concrete sub-floor. These can be removed (though more may appear) by washing the tiles with a white vinegar solution (75ml vinegar to 5 litres water). Do not rinse off the solution and do not polish the tiles until the white patches cease to appear.

**Rubber**  Never use a synthetic detergent or solvent-based wax polish as rubber flooring is easily softened. Wash with a soapflake solution, rinse, dry and apply an emulsion polish.

If the floor is textured be careful not to let polish build up in the cracks.

**Stone**  Stone floors should be swept regularly and washed from time to time with a solution of washing soda (a handful to a bucket of warm water).

If your stone floor is in a kitchen or dining-room where greasy spills occur, it is a good idea to *seal* the stone in order to make cleaning easier and to prevent stains being absorbed. Before sealing ensure that the floor has been thoroughly cleaned; anything left on the surface will remain fixed under the sealant.

---

When cleaning floors of any material, do not use a cellulose mop with bleach solution – this will cause the mop to disintegrate.

---

**Tiles** See 'Ceramic tiles', 'Cork tiles' and 'Quarry tiles', pages 90–92.

**Vinyl** Vinyl flooring will need less frequent washing if swept regularly. Mop with warm water (add a little household cleaner and rinse with clear water if the floor is dirty), and when the floor is dry apply an emulsion polish (a solvent-based wax polish will damage the surface).

When the emulsion polish starts to build up, remove it with the manufacturer's recommended product and start again from scratch.

**Wood** *Waxed wood* flooring should be swept with a soft broom and dry-mopped to remove dust and loose soil. Sticky marks can be removed with a damp cloth wrung out in clean water. Waxed wood should *not* be washed, as water can distort the wood. Apply a coating of wax polish paste with fine grain steel wool from time to time. When the polish builds up to an unacceptable level (i.e. when the floor starts to feel and look sticky), remove the old wax with a cloth dipped in white spirit. Allow to dry thoroughly before applying a new coating of wax.

*Sealed wood* floors should be damp-mopped to remove dust. Apply a coating of wax or emulsion polish from time to time for added shine.

> Sprinkle damp tea leaves or torn-up damp strips of paper on to a dusty wooden floor before sweeping. This will prevent the dust from rising – useful if you are asthmatic – and make it easier to clean up.

## Upholstery

Upholstery should not need to be cleaned very often. Treat stains when they occur, dust regularly with the appropriate vacuum cleaner tool and be sure to do any major cleaning before the fabric gets too dirty.

*Fixed covers*   Clean these in position. If the fabric is expensive you may wish to call in a professional firm. Otherwise vacuum or brush the furniture, then use an upholstery shampoo, following the instructions supplied. Note that Dralon can react badly to some upholstery shampoos. Whatever the fabric, test the shampoo first for colour change on an inconspicuous part. When it has dried thoroughly, vacuum or brush again to remove any shampoo residue and the dirt it has absorbed.

*Leather covers* should be cleaned by sponging with a damp cloth wiped over a tablet of glycerine soap. Do not over-wet. Wipe with a clean damp cloth but do not worry about getting out all the soap; it helps to keep the leather supple. Apply a thin coating of hide food from time to time and buff well so that it does not rub off on to clothes.

*Plastic and vinyl covers* should be wiped with warm soapy water, then with clean water, and buffed with a soft cloth. If the furniture has a wooden frame take care not to wet it as the colour may rub off on to the vinyl or plastic.

Wash in the same way as curtains (see overleaf). **Loose covers**
Most loose covers will be too bulky to fit into a
domestic washing-machine and will have to be
hand-washed.

Loose covers will shrink slightly as they dry
and should be put back on furniture while still
slightly damp so that they can be stretched into
the correct position. Iron with the covers in
position.

*Glazed cotton covers* can be hand-washed gently
in warm water, but do not wring or rub.
Squeeze out moisture or spin-dry briefly and
dry. Iron on the non-glazed side, using the cotton setting.

---

If cushion covers can be displayed either way
round, turn them once a week to stop them
fading in sunlight.

---

Embroidery should not be washed, treated with **Embroidered**
upholstery shampoo or any dry-cleaning prod- **covers**
uct. Keep it free from dust by using a soft vacuum cleaner attachment on a low suction level.
Fixed chair or stool seats with beading or raised
threadwork of any kind are best brushed gently
by hand with a baby's hairbrush.

Valuable embroidery should be cleaned professionally. The Royal School of Needlework
(see 'Textiles' in Addresses section) will be able
to do this or advise on a specialist firm in your
area. If you need embroidery removed from
chair or stool seats for cleaning, contact a professional upholsterer or consult the Royal
School of Needlework.

# Curtains

In theory, many curtain fabrics can be washed at home; however, you should remember that any lining or interlining may shrink at a different rate from the main fabric. Even the thread with which the curtains are sewn may shrink at a different rate and cause problems along the seams. If you have spent a lot of money on your curtains or a lot of time making them yourself it is probably better to have them cleaned professionally (see page 19 for advice on employing contract cleaners). Fancy finishes such as swags and tails should also be dry-cleaned.

*Looking after curtains*

Dust regularly using the soft brush attachment of your vacuum cleaner or a soft long-handled brush. Brushes with synthetic fibre bristles create static and are particularly good for collecting dust. It is also a good idea – provided you are sure you can rehang them correctly – to hang curtains outdoors on a dry breezy day.

*Washing and drying curtains*

- Follow the instructions supplied with the fabric.
- If you intend to machine-wash your curtains make sure that the dry weight fits comfortably in the drum; thick fabrics will become very heavy when wet.
- Measure the curtains before you wash them so that you can stretch them to the correct size afterwards. If you are worried about shrinkage, take down the hems before washing.
- Remove hooks and any weights and loosen the curtain tapes so that the curtains lie flat; if the curtain pleats are stitched in, dry-clean.
- Shake well to remove dust and run the soft brush attachment of the vacuum cleaner over each side. (Curtains will pick up less dust if this is done on a bed, not on the floor.)
- Soak curtains in a bathful of cold water to remove loose dirt, then either hand- or machine-wash according to the fabric

instructions. In general, hand-washing is preferable since fabrics may be damaged by the harsher action of a machine.

- If hand-washing, do not rub or wring the fabric, just agitate it gently with your hands. Rinse thoroughly and either squeeze or spin-dry.

- Hang to dry over two parallel washing-lines. This may involve some improvisation with airers, chairbacks, etc. Make sure that the wet fabric does not touch any wood, which could stain it.

- While still just damp, iron the curtains on the wrong side, working along the vertical length. If some parts of the fabric have dried, dampen the whole curtain so that water marking does not occur.

- As you iron, stretch the seams gently to remove any puckering. When you have finished, spread out the curtain on a clean flat surface, perhaps a bed, and pull to the correct size.

- When the curtains are dry, insert hooks and weights and pull the tape to the correct width before rehanging.

> Rehanging heavy curtains is best done by two people: one on a stepladder fixing the hooks, the other keeping the weight and bulk of the fabric off the ground.

*Net curtains*

Net curtains should be washed on a regular basis *before* they start to look grubby. If dirt is visible, permanent discoloration may occur. Soak in cold water first to remove loose dirt, then wash. There is usually no need to iron, so rehang while still slightly damp and pull into shape.

**Curtain rails**  Clean while curtains are being washed. Stand on a steady stepladder and use the crevice tool attachment of a vacuum cleaner to remove dust from the rail and from behind it.

*Brass and brass-effect curtain rails* are lacquered and just need a thorough dusting.

*Plastic rails* should be washed in a solution of washing-up liquid, then rinsed in clear water. Either sponge the rails in position or take them down and clean in the bath. Gliders should be removed from the rail and soaked in a bowl of washing-up liquid solution, then rinsed. When tracks are clean and dry, spray the channel with an aerosol lubricant to ensure smooth running. Leave to dry before rehanging curtains.

*Wooden rails* should be dusted and given a light coating of polish. Rub it in well so that no residue is absorbed by the curtain fabric.

---

**Curtain cords** should be kept dry, if possible, as they could shrink. Run a duster over them to remove loose dirt.

---

**Pelmets**  *Fabric pelmets* If the pelmet is firmly fixed to the wall, brush regularly with the upholstery attachment of a vacuum cleaner. If it is dirty apply a little upholstery shampoo, taking care not to affect the shape. If the pelmet can be taken down, dry-clean or wash according to the fabric. Always use a dry-cleaner if the pelmet is lined, as the lining may shrink at a different rate from the main fabric. Give the dry-cleaner the pelmet measurements so that he or she can ensure it comes back the right size.

*Wooden pelmets* Dust with the crevice tool of your vacuum cleaner if you can reach, otherwise dust manually. Use a spray polish, and a cotton bud to get into any nooks where dirt has built up.

*Plastic pelmets* Wipe these over with a warm detergent solution, then rinse and buff dry.

Make sure all pelmets are dry before you re-hang curtains.

> Take advantage of curtains or blinds being down to clean the window embrasure thoroughly, including the inside of the glass and the windowsill. If polishing wooden windowsills, buff thoroughly so that no polish residue rubs off on to the hem of the curtain.

## Blinds

Blinds should be cleaned according to their structure and fabric, as described below.

**Bamboo**

Use the upholstery attachment of a vacuum cleaner or a feather duster to remove dust from between the bamboo slats. Occasionally take the blind down, spread it out flat and wipe over with a cloth wrung out of a solution of washing-up liquid. Rinse with a clean damp cloth, taking care not to over-wet and distort the bamboo. Allow to dry naturally, away from direct heat.

**Canvas**

If possible, take down the blind and spread out on a clean surface outdoors (a patio or garden table covered with plastic sheeting). Scrub with a soft brush and detergent solution and rinse in cold water. Dry thoroughly before refixing. Canvas which is used outside can be treated with a water-proofing solution (available from camping shops).

**Festoon (Austrian)**

Vacuum with a dusting attachment to prevent dirt settling in the folds. To clean the blind, take it down, loosen the vertical tapes until it is flat, then wash or dry-clean according to the fabric.

**Pleated paper**  Dust frequently to prevent dirt from building up in the creases. Use a little neat washing-up liquid to remove bad marks. Never immerse in water; wipe over with a damp cloth wrung out in clear warm water, taking care not to over-wet.

**Roller**  Dust regularly, using the soft brush attachment of the vacuum cleaner. Pay particular attention to the roller springs, where a build-up of dust can cause malfunction. From time to time take the blind down, lie it flat and vacuum each side. *Spongeable fabric* should be wiped over with a weak solution of washing-up liquid followed by a clean water rinse. Dry flat. You may wish to apply a coating of aerosol blind stiffener/protector. This is best done outdoors on a still day by pegging the blind to a clothes line.
*Non-spongeable fabric* Remove marks with an india rubber.

**Roman**  Dust regularly with a vacuum cleaner dusting attachment. Always dry-clean, as an exact right-angled finished shape is critical to the blinds' appearance.

**Venetian**  Venetian blinds are difficult to dust conventionally. You can buy a special two- or three-pronged brush which cleans more than one slat at a time, or use the dusting attachment of a vacuum cleaner. Alternatively, buy a pair of soft cotton cleaning gloves and do the job with your hands.

Wipe over the slats occasionally with a weak solution of household detergent, then buff to a shine. (Wear protective gloves while doing this as the slats can cut your hands.) Wipe down the tapes with the same solution, then with clear water. Dry with the blinds hanging full-length so that the tapes do not shrink.

If a kitchen blind has accumulated a build-up of grease, take it down and clean it in the bath, first laying down an old towel to protect the bath's surface. Wash in warm soapy water, then rinse, taking care to keep the roller mechanism dry. Hang up immediately, wipe down the tapes with a dry cloth and leave at full length until the tapes are dry. Venetian blinds will stay cleaner for longer if you apply a coating of anti-static polish.

## Walls and ceilings

Walls and ceilings should not be overlooked when you undertake a major clean of your home. Clear the room of as much clutter as possible and put dustsheets over any furniture that cannot be moved. Try to move items away from the walls so that you can work more quickly and efficiently.

### Painted walls

Dust and then wash with a solution of washing-up liquid. Do not use other cleaning products as these can alter the colour of the paint.

If walls are very dirty, use either a weak solution of sugar soap or a diluted general-purpose household cleaner applied on a cellulose sponge or an absorbent cloth. Wash one section of the wall at a time – about one square metre – then rinse with clean water. Overlap the sections slightly to avoid tidemarks.

---

Wash walls from the bottom upwards as any dirty streaks which dribble down as you work are much easier to wipe off a clean surface than a dirty one. Clean really dirty patches with undiluted cleaning solution.

---

Do not stop when you have started to wash a wall, otherwise a tidemark will form between the clean and the dirty part which may be difficult to remove.

If you are washing a wall that has light switches or electrical sockets, make sure the electricity supply is turned off and be careful not to get water in them.

---

**Discoloured walls above radiators**
Wallcoverings can be discoloured by dust rising in the hot air currents from radiators. To prevent this from happening, fit shelves above your radiators.

---

*Wallpaper*  Wallpaper is easily damaged so work gently. Dust with a soft brush or the soft brush attachment of the vacuum cleaner. Take care not to flatten the pattern on textured wallpaper by pressing too hard.

Do not wash wallpaper as the colours may run and the paper become detached from the wall. Clean soiled patches with a soft, clean india rubber or a chunk of crustless white bread.

*Vinyl wallcovering*  Wash with a mild detergent solution and rinse with clean water. Take care not to over-wet the vinyl and avoid getting cleaning solution in the joins. Clean from the bottom upwards.

*Grasscloth wallcovering*  This is difficult to clean as the grasses easily work loose. Use a soft brush vacuum cleaner attachment on low suction. Treat marks with an aerosol grease solvent. Avoid putting furniture against grasscloth as it rubs the grasses loose and leaves marks.

Clean regularly with a vacuum cleaner attachment, as the texture attracts dust. The dyes used in hessian wallcovering tend to run so do not wet or use stain-removal products. Treat marks with a chunk of crustless white bread.

**Hessian wallcovering**

Dust regularly with either a ceiling brush or a vacuum cleaner attachment.

**Wood panelling**

*Sealed panelling* just needs wiping with a cloth wrung out in a mild detergent solution. Rinse with clean water and buff dry immediately. Maintain the shine with occasional use of an aerosol cleaner or polish.

*Wax-finished panelling* should be polished with a good-quality wax paste once or twice a year. When the wax builds up and starts to smear and show fingerprints you should remove it with white spirit and re-apply. White spirit applied on fine steel wool and rubbed in the direction of the grain will also improve the appearance of faded and scratched panelling. Polish and buff.

Clean with an aerosol cleaner/polish. Badly soiled areas should be washed with a solution of washing-up liquid, then rinsed in clean water.

**Painted wood**

*Painted skirting boards* should be washed with a solution of washing-up liquid, rinsed and dried. If they are very dirty, wash first with sugar soap. Do not use household cleaners, which may affect the colour of the paint.

**Skirting boards**

*Unpainted wooden skirting boards* should be dusted, then given a light coating of aerosol cleaner/polish.

To clean wall switches first make a template from thin card so that the cleaning product does not get on the wall. Then clean according to the

**Light fittings**

material. For plastic switches use either an aerosol cleaner/polish or, if badly finger-marked, a little methylated spirit applied on a soft cloth. On metal fittings, use metal polish.

Clean plastic electrical sockets with methylated spirit, having switched off the electricity at the mains and taking care not to get any liquid in the holes.

**Ceilings**   Ceilings should not get very dirty unless there are smokers in the house or there is a coal fire in the room. To clean high ceilings use a step-ladder with wide steps, a rail to hold on to and a platform for your cleaning tools; and, ideally, protective goggles and a nose and mouth mask.

Use either a long-handled ceiling brush or a vacuum cleaner dusting attachment. You can make your own ceiling brush by tying a clean duster over the head of a soft-bristled broom.

Do not bother to wash ceilings. A fresh coat of paint is more effective.

# Fireplaces

If you have a real fire in your home the fireplace is likely to become soiled with soot and smoke. It will be more difficult to clean if you let the dirt build up than if you tackle it regularly.

**Brick**   Brick fireplaces quickly become ingrained with dirt, so brush the bricks regularly with a soft brush or vacuum cleaner attachment.

When dirt has built up, first try scrubbing with a hard brush and clean warm water. If this fails, scrub with neat white malt vinegar, then rinse. Do not use soap or detergent as they may be absorbed by the bricks and be very difficult to remove.

*Heavy staining* can be remedied with a solution of spirit of salts (one part to six parts water) but bear in mind that this is an extremely corrosive chemical and should not come into contact with your hands or clothes. Always wear protective goggles and make sure the room is well ventilated.

## Cast iron

*Rust build-up* can be removed with a wire brush or steel wool; make sure your eyes are protected. Take care not to damage any intricate decoration by brushing or rubbing too hard. Use a proprietary non-drip rust remover to get rid of any remaining residue, ensuring that you follow the manufacturer's instructions for application and neutralising.

To prevent further rust build-up, apply a thin layer of oil (vegetable oil is preferable as it has no smell).

## Marble

Sponge with a weak solution of soapflakes, rinse and buff dry. If the fireplace has a polished finish, apply a marble polish but avoid the areas that get hot.

If marble has become worn or chipped, special products to improve its appearance are available.

## Slate

*Smooth slate* Wipe over with a cloth wrung out well in washing-up liquid. Rinse with a cloth dipped sparingly in clean water and buff with a soft cloth. A marble polish (see above) will give it a good sheen but should not be used on areas affected by heat.

*Riven slate* If the rough surface attracts soot, scrub with a brush and a solution of washing-up liquid.

**Stone**   Sponge with clean warm water (the sponge will prevent soot from being absorbed into the stone). Where soiling is heavy, use a scrubbing brush and, if necessary, a solution of washing-up liquid. Do not use soap or scouring powder, which may alter the colour of the stone.

If you inherit a badly soiled stone fireplace, scrub it with a solution of bleach (one cup to a bucketful of water) but be sure to protect the floor, the surroundings and yourself.

**Ceramic tiles**   Wash well with a solution of washing-up liquid. *Scorch marks* should come off with a non-abrasive household cleaner applied on a cloth (a brush can damage the glaze). Do not wipe the tiles when they are hot, otherwise the glaze may crack. Apply an aerosol cleaner/polish to prevent further soiling, then buff well.

**Fire irons**   Clean according to the metal they are made from (see 'Metals', page 123). When cooled down after use in a fire, wipe off coal dust and soot with a damp cloth to prevent it building up and looking unsightly.

# Chapter 4
# Particular articles and materials

## Around the house

There are certain fittings and ornaments in every household that are neglected when it comes to cleaning. Often it is a case of not knowing what is the best method of cleaning to use – although some items are so commonplace we simply forget to clean them. Valuable articles and mechanical objects are usually best left in the hands of an expert.

*Basketware*   Use a brush or vacuum cleaner attachment (set at a low suction level) to remove dust. Wipe over with a damp cloth and allow to dry naturally.

*Books*   Books are easily neglected as on the whole they do not show dirt. None the less, they do need care – even paperbacks. Take one book at a time and first blow, then dust, along the top with a soft cloth or feather duster while holding the book firmly closed to prevent dust slipping between the pages. Use an india rubber to remove surface dirt from any pages. Leather-bound books need special treatment to prevent their covers from cracking. Make up a soap solution by whisking a tablet of glycerine soap in warm water until a lather forms. Wipe this over the leather with a barely damp cloth. Place the book on a clean white towel to dry naturally, then apply a thin coating of hide food. Valuable books should be checked regularly for any signs of deterioration and taken to a specialist book-seller or museum for advice or attention.

*Bookshelves*   If you do not have time to clean bookshelves thoroughly, running the crevice tool of a vacuum cleaner along the front of the shelves not covered by books will remove a good amount of surface dust and should not damage most books (however, do not do this if the books are very old or valuable).

Glass-fronted bookshelves are a good idea if you have a lot of books and not much time to clean. Alternatively, ask a local leather supplier if you can get strips of leather to fix along the top edge of the shelves; this keeps dust from falling on to the tops of the books. An antiquarian book dealer should be able to put you in touch with a supplier (see 'Books' in Addresses section.) Use a polish suitable for the shelf surfaces, making sure that it is well rubbed in and will not come off on the books. If you find that books are infested with bookworm, first clean the shelves, then use an insecticidal spray. Finally, use a polish containing an anti-woodworm element.

**Candlesticks**

To remove dried wax, first chip off the excess. With silver and other metal candlesticks, hold upside down and dip in boiling water to melt any remaining wax. On wooden and plastic candlesticks use a hair-dryer to melt the wax. Take care not to overheat wood or it may crack.

Clean according to the material – see relevant sections within this chapter.

**Clocks**

Clocks should be cleaned professionally (see *Yellow Pages* for local clock repairers). Dust and polish the exterior of longcase (grandfather) clocks but take care not to touch the weights inside. Do not clean the face. Wipe over any glass with methylated spirit; this also applies to the glass of carriage clocks. Old and valuable clocks should be covered with a plastic bag while you are dusting the room.

**Doormats**

See page 170.

**Fountain pens**

Clean a fountain pen from time to time by taking it apart and soaking the bits in vinegar. Dry them on kitchen paper before reassembling.

**Flowers**   ***Dried (and artificial) flowers*** These can be dusted using a hair-dryer on the lowest setting.
***Silk flowers*** Use either a feather duster or the cool setting of a hair dryer to remove dust from silk flowers. On no account wet them, otherwise the texture will be ruined. Clean them fairly regularly to prevent dust building up to a level that is difficult to remove.

**House plants**   Dirty house plants will not thrive. Spray soft-leaved plants with clear water unless the care instructions preclude this. Dust shiny-leaved plants with a soft cloth, then sponge with clean water or, very occasionally, use a leaf-shining product. Always use water at room temperature rather than cold.

**Lampshades**   Keep free from dust so that as much light as possible can shine through. Dust lampshades regularly when you are cleaning a room and treat according to the fabric when they become dirty.
***Buckram lampshades*** may need brushing with a stiff brush if dust has become ingrained. Clean with a soft cloth dipped in turpentine, rubbing over the whole surface to avoid a patchy finish.
***Parchment lampshades*** Real parchment dissolves if wetted. (However, the parchment is usually an imitation and made from plastic.) Dust gently and remove marks with an india rubber.
***Plastic lampshades*** may be fully washable, in which case clean in soapy water, rinse in clean water and dry thoroughly – otherwise the metal in the frame may rust. To be quite sure to avoid rusting, use a sponge instead of immersing the lampshade.
***Vellum lampshades*** Using a screw-top jar, shake together one part soapflakes, one part

warm water and two parts methylated spirit. Wipe this over the lampshade, then rinse with a cloth dipped in neat methylated spirit. Apply a thin coating of wax furniture polish, rubbing in carefully.

**Pleated lampshades** Remove dust by dabbing with double-width sticky tape.

**Locks**

If you polish locks to keep them looking nice, try to avoid getting polish in the works. Use a general-purpose lubricant occasionally and, if you have difficulty getting keys in, gently insert a sharp lead pencil into the keyhole: the graphite will make the movement easier.

**Oil lamps**

The delicate glass chimneys of oil lamps are inclined to crack when washed. Use newspaper to wipe out the inside when it becomes coated with smoke. You can reduce smokiness by soaking the wick in vinegar when it is new, and trimming the wick off evenly after each use.

**Papier mâché**

Dust regularly. Clean occasionally: wipe over occasionally with a cloth wrung out in soapy water, then wipe with clean water and immediately pat dry. Protect with a thin application of furniture cream.

**Perspex**

Perspex scratches easily but light marks can be removed by rubbing over with a little metal polish in a circular movement. Clean with a solution of washing-up liquid, rinse off and dry. A light squirt from a spray cleaner/polish will help to maintain shine.

Other rigid plastics can be treated in the same way as Perspex.

**Pictures**

Because acrylic and oil paintings are not covered with glass they are particularly prone to

111

discoloration by smoke from open fires and cigarettes. Watercolours and prints may be bought unframed and, if old, may have marks.

*Acrylic paintings* Do not attempt to clean these yourself but go to an expert (see *Yellow Pages* or ask in your local framing shop).

For everyday care use a feather duster flicked gently over the surface unless the picture is valuable or has obviously loose flecks of paint, in which case leave well alone. In general, hang acrylic pictures where they will not be affected by smoke.

*Oil paintings* Dust carefully using either a very soft cloth or a fluffy long-handled brush, taking care not to touch the canvas with the handle. Valuable oil paintings should be cleaned professionally. Alternatively, you can buy special picture-cleaner from art shops. If the painting is varnished, cleaning will remove this and you will need to have the picture re-varnished.

*Prints and watercolours* Have these professionally treated if of monetary or sentimental value. Grease marks can be removed with an acetone solvent (available from art shops) applied on a soft cloth. Cover the mark with blotting paper and apply the tip of a warm iron to draw out the stain.

**Picture frames**  *Gilded picture frames* need frequent dusting. Use the soft attachment of a vacuum cleaner on intricately carved frames, and cotton buds to reach into deep crevices. If discoloration occurs rub over the whole frame with a cloth dipped in turpentine substitute. You can touch up damaged spots with gilt wax (available from art shops) but the damage may still show. This treatment is not advisable for valuable frames. For gold leaf, see page 127.

*Plastic picture frames* should be wiped over with a damp cloth. Use neat washing-up liquid on any marks.

***Wood frames*** should be dusted regularly. Polish occasionally with a little furniture cream, rubbed in well.

*Radiators* Use a vacuum cleaner tool to clean the front and top and as far behind as possible. Some fluffy brushes are narrow enough to use behind radiators; otherwise unwind a wire coat-hanger, make a loop at the end and tie a duster over it to do the job. Dirty painted radiators can be washed in a solution of heavy-duty household cleaner, but check on a test patch first that this will not affect colour.

*Trays* Even if regularly wiped or washed, trays tend to build up dirt around the edges. Use a blunt knife to get this out. With antique and valuable trays be careful not to damage the surface.

*Umbrellas* Drain a wet umbrella by standing it on its side, fully open, in a warm room – but not too close to a heat source. To clean umbrellas – particularly golf umbrellas, which tend to get dirty – wipe over with a weak solution of washing-up liquid applied on a clean cloth.

## Furniture

Looking after furniture, even antique furniture, is less trouble than many people imagine. *Dusting* is the key to keeping it clean. *Polishing* needs to be done only infrequently, and most modern furniture finishes just need an occasional wipe-over. It is important to know what your furniture is made from. Keep care labels when you buy it new and try to obtain as much information as possible about any older furniture you may acquire, particularly if it is valuable.

> Do not keep valuable furniture in bright sunlight, as this will damage its appearance.

*Antique*   Even though it has survived the ravages of time, antique furniture can easily be destroyed by central heating. Keep the room temperature at around 18°C/65°F and place a humidifier or bowl of water in the room. Don't place antiques near radiators.

On the whole, experts do not recommend polishes which contain silicones, as they produce an unnatural finish. Use a good-quality non-silicone polish once or twice a year, buffing well to prevent a sticky build-up. Otherwise just dust and remove any greasy marks with a chamois leather wrung out in a vinegar solution (one part white vinegar to eight parts water). Antique furniture can also be cleaned professionally (see 'Antiques' in Addresses section).

---

**How to make your own silicone-free wax polish**

You will need:

- 50g beeswax (available from craft and candle-making shops; the local library should also have a list of beekeepers)
- 125ml turpentine (not turpentine substitute)

Grate or chop the beeswax into a screw-top jar and add the turpentine. Stand the jar in a bowl of hot water until the wax melts. Screw on the lid and shake well. Use in very small quantities – a little goes a long way.

---

*Painted wood*   Clean with a solution of washing-up liquid. Check on a small test area first to make sure this will not affect the finish. (If it does, clean by dusting only.)

*Sealed wood*   Dust regularly and wipe over with a damp cloth from time to time. A spray with cleaner or polish will maintain shine.

Treat as antique furniture (see opposite). **Waxed wood**

> Never mix different polishes on the same piece of furniture: a chemical reaction may occur.

Never treat with traditional furniture polish; dust and, once or twice a year, apply a proprietary oil. **Oiled wood**

Remove sticky marks with a cloth wrung out well in warm soapy water. Where polish has built up (test by seeing if a finger leaves a print) remove with white spirit. Polish occasionally with good wax polish; otherwise just dust. If damaged by scratches or spills, have the piece re-polished professionally. **French-polished wood**

Teak should maintain a matt finish and be polished with a special teak cream or oil only once or twice a year. Rub well to ensure no sticky residue remains to attract dust. Dust regularly. **Teak**

Dust with a vacuum cleaner attachment or a soft brush. If dirt is visible add 10ml laundry borax to a bowl of warm soapy water and clean with a scrubbing-brush. Rinse in warm salted water (10ml salt to 1 litre water) to stiffen and bleach the bamboo. Wipe dry, then apply a little furniture cream. **Bamboo**

Remove dust with a brush or vacuum cleaner attachment. **Cane**
*Unvarnished cane* If dirty, rub with fine-gauge steel wool dampened in a solution of warm water and washing soda. Wipe over with cold water to rinse and stiffen the cane. Do not allow it to get very wet as this will soften it.
*Varnished cane* just needs wiping over with a damp cloth.

**Leather**   Dust regularly. Dirt should be removed with a damp cloth which has been thoroughly wrung out in warm water and rubbed over a tablet of glycerine soap. Do not rinse, as leaving a little soap on the leather will help to keep it soft and supple. Apply a little hide food from time to time to help prevent cracking and stains. Rub this in well so that it does not come off on clothes.

*Imitation hides* Sponge with a lukewarm soapflake solution (never detergent), then rinse with clear water and dry with a clean cloth. Buff with a soft duster.

*Leather desk-tops* If ink is spilled, wipe it off immediately with tepid water on a clean soft cloth. For ballpoint ink use milk rather than water, then clean the whole leather area. If the surface is washable, use a damp cloth which has been rubbed over a tablet of glycerine soap. Leave to dry (the glycerine feeds the leather), then apply a thin coating of hide food. Apply hide food reasonably often to protect against stains.

**Upholstery**   See page 94.

**Glass**   See 'Furniture', page 123.

**Plastic**   An occasional wipe with a detergent solution followed by rinsing should be sufficient. Use an aerosol cleaner/polish to maintain shine and protect against dust.

**Ormolu**   See page 131.

**Lloyd Loom**   This type of furniture is made by winding fabric round wire. It is no longer manufactured and items now command good prices.

Remove dust with a hair-dryer on its cool setting. Clean with a warm washing-up liquid solution, using a soft brush and taking care not to over-wet. Rinse with a cloth wrung out in warm water. Leave to dry naturally.

Pianos with a polyester finish need a specialist product available from music shops (see also 'Pianos' in Addresses section). French-polished pianos should be cleaned as described on page 115.

**Pianos**

*Ivory* piano keys can be cleaned by wiping with a solution of methylated spirit and warm water (equal parts) applied on just-damp cotton wool balls. Badly discoloured keys need to be professionally scraped and re-polished. Otherwise just dust, then wipe over with a chamois leather wrung out in warm water containing a few drops of white vinegar. Be careful not to let any liquid trickle down between the keys. Wipe dry.

Leaving the piano lid open on sunny days will stop keys from yellowing. Seek professional advice for valuable instruments.

*Plastic* piano keys should be dusted regularly and cleaned with a chamois leather wrung out in warm water with a few drops of white malt vinegar added. Wipe dry. Plastic keys do not discolour.

Dust inside the case of the piano using the crevice tool attachment of a vacuum cleaner, avoiding the strings. For uprights, remove the bottom panel and vacuum away any fluff which has collected on the felt.

> A piano should be kept in a room that is neither too dry nor too humid. Consult your piano-tuner for advice. Avoid fluctuations in temperature and keep heating below 22°C/72°F. Do not place a piano near windows, radiators or damp walls.

## First aid for wood

Wood is easily marked or damaged, but polish is not usually the answer. Getting marks out depends on what has caused them, so use one of the following treatments as appropriate.

*Alcohol marks*   Rub along the grain with cream metal polish.

*Bruising*   Remove the finish with paint/varnish removers. Soak a piece of white blotting paper in water and fold to form a pad. Place over the mark and leave for 12 hours or overnight; cover with clingfilm so the pad does not dry out. This should make the wood grain swell. Remove the blotting paper and allow to dry naturally. Sand gently, following the grain. When smooth, finish the surface with an appropriate varnishing product. This treatment is not suitable for french-polished wood and should not be used on valuable antiques.

*Dents*   *Solid wood* raise the dent by leaving a little warm water in the hollow. If this does not work, remove the wax finish with white spirit. Follow the instructions above for bruising, applying the tip of a warm iron to the blotting paper. When the wood has dried out use a wood colourstick or shoe polish to correct the colour.
*Veneered wood* This will need patching. Buy a small piece of matching veneer from a craft shop that stocks marquetry sets, or from a furniture restorer. Trim it to a size that will cover the damaged area comfortably, making sure the grain runs the same way as the rest of the veneer. Place it over the dent and with a sharp craft knife cut an oval through both sections. Lift off the patch and remove the damaged veneer with a narrow wood chisel or a blunt knife. You may need to wet it to soften the glue. Clean any glue residue from the area.

Dampen the new veneer to make it flexible. Apply wood adhesive and press into position, wiping off any surplus adhesive. Smooth into position using the rounded handle of a screwdriver. Place a piece of brown paper over the repair and weigh it down. Leave to dry thoroughly, then smooth the edges of the patch with fine abrasive paper and use a wood colourstick or shoe polish to restore colour. Buff well.

**Burns**

Treat slight burns with cream metal polish, rubbing along the grain. Where a burn has roughened a solid wood surface, use a very sharp knife to scrape the surface, then sand with very fine abrasive paper and apply the wet blotting paper remedy described earlier under 'Bruising'.

If the burn is deep, scrape with a sharp craft knife until the hole is clean. Use a matching shade of wood filler to fill the hole, smoothing it level with the surface. When dry, take a very fine artist's paintbrush and paint in the grain using artists' oil or watercolour paint of the right shade.

**Cigarette burns** Rub down with fine steel wool, then rub in a little linseed oil and leave overnight before polishing.

**Heat marks**

These appear white in colour. Rub in the direction of the grain with a cream metal polish.

**Ink stains**

Use a cotton wool bud dipped in bleach, then dry quickly with kitchen paper. Re-apply as necessary. For large stains, remove the wood finish then use a proprietary wood bleach. Use a wood colourstick or shoe polish to restore colour before refinishing.

**Scratches**

Use a wood colourstick, wax crayon or shoe polish.

*Water marks*  Rub along the grain with cream metal polish. If the surface is rough, rub with very fine steel wool dipped in liquid wax polish.

## Glass

A smeary end-result is what most people want to avoid when cleaning glass. A perfect finish will depend very much upon the article being cleaned.

*Windows*  Always clean windows on dull days: sunlight dries them too quickly, producing smears. How often you clean the outside will very much depend on the area in which you live; the inside should be cleaned at least twice a year.

Many modern windows are of the 'tip and tilt' variety which makes them easy to clean both on the inside and on the outside and cuts out the need for using a ladder. When cleaning windows, loop curtains through a hanger to keep them out of the way.

A proprietary window-cleaning product is best. Use sprays and aerosols for small areas and leaded lights. Alternatively, add either 100g laundry borax or 30ml vinegar to a small bucket of warm water and clean with a chamois leather. A 'wiper' blade is useful for tackling expanses of glass in clean sweeps and should be wiped after each stroke.

---

- Buff up clean dry glass with crumpled newspaper; the ink will add shine.
- Use an old toothbrush and a proprietary mould cleaner to get rid of black mould growing in window corners.

---

Clean with a proprietary glass-cleaning product. *Mirrors*
In rooms such as bathrooms and kitchens where
mirrors tend to mist over, use a product
designed for car windscreens containing an anti-
mist chemical, such as Clear-shield (see Chapter
9, Products that work). Never use water when
cleaning a mirror: it can get between the glass
and the silvering behind it and cause staining.
This applies equally to modern bathroom cabinet mirrors and valuable antiques.

Everyday drinking glasses can be washed by *Drinking*
hand in warm washing-up liquid or in a dish- *glasses*
washer. Rinse, drain and polish with a soft, non-
fluffy cloth. Always use fresh water and wash
separately from crockery and cutlery. Use a
plastic bowl to prevent them knocking against
the hard surface of a sink and take care not to
chip glasses on taps.

*Cut glass and fine crystal* should be washed by
hand in warm washing-up liquid; repeated
washing in a dishwasher will cause 'etching' –
the build-up of white marking caused by strong
detergent which is impossible to remove. Take
care when drying stemmed glasses that you do
not twist the stem too hard and break it away
from the bowl.

---

- Good-quality glasses should be stored
  upright as the rim is the easiest part to
  damage.
- Do not stack cut-glass or crystal tumblers
  inside each other.

---

Put a towel in the sink when washing delicate
items such as glassware.

---

**Carafes and decanters**  Try to rinse out immediately after use as these will become stained if dregs are left in them for any length of time. The traditional method of cleaning is to roll lead shot around the base; an equally effective and simpler solution is to soak the inside in a warm solution of biological detergent or to mix up enough white malt vinegar and salt to cover the base. Leave either mixture for several hours, shaking at intervals. Rinse thoroughly with warm water until the smell of alcohol has disappeared and stand the glassware upside down in a jug to drain. Some ships' decanters have very wide bases and are not safe to turn upside down. If you use one regularly, invest in a fabric tube filled with moisture-absorbing crystals or drain in a bucket padded with a towel.

**Chandeliers**  Valuable glass chandeliers should be taken to pieces, cleaned and re-assembled by an expert – unless you are *absolutely* confident of your ability to do it yourself. If you do decide to have a go, remember first to switch off the electricity at the mains. Remove each piece of glass individually, wash it in a solution of washing-up liquid with a few drops of ammonia, rinse, drain on a non-fluffy cloth and polish with a chamois leather. You will need to be sure of how the various pieces fit together again; either follow the manufacturer's instructions or draw your own diagram.

To clean a chandelier without taking it down from the ceiling, use a step-ladder and rub over each piece with dry chamois leather gloves. Also available is chandelier aerosol, which you spray at the glass and allow to dry before polishing with a chamois leather or a soft cloth. If you use this method be sure to protect the floor below with plastic sheeting.

See pages 166 and 172.

**Conservatories and greenhouses**

Items such as glass-fronted bookcases and cupboards and glass-topped tables should be cleaned with a proprietary window cleaner, or an aerosol cleaner or polish. Bad smears can be removed with methylated spirit applied on a cotton wool ball. Buff well, taking care that the cloth you use is completely free from grit.

**Furniture**

See page 55.

**Oven doors**

> Clean scratches from watch-glass faces by rubbing gently with a cloth dipped in metal polish.

Light bulbs will give off better light if cleaned every couple of months. Switch off the light and remove the bulb (wait until it is cool if necessary). Hold it at the fixing end and wipe over the glass with a barely damp cloth. Dry with a soft, non-fluffy cloth and replace. Fluorescent lighting tubes can be cleaned using the same method.

**Light bulbs**

## Metals

Metals of one sort or another are found throughout the home, with a variety of uses from the functional to ornamental. An all-purpose metal cleaner is suitable for some, while others respond better to a specific cleaner. Never clean valuable items, as this could affect their sale price.

> Clean small metal items such as coins by dunking them in fizzy cola for a few minutes.

**Aluminium**    See 'Aluminium pans', page 66.

**Brass**    Brass should be cleaned with a proprietary metal polish. Using a 'long-term' variety will leave a film on the surface that reduces the build-up of tarnish.

Slightly tarnished brass can be cleaned with a paste made from salt and lemon juice. Use a soft toothbrush to clean out any crevices.

Where there is a build-up of old metal polish on patterned brass, rub the affected area gently with very fine steel wool (gauge 0000), then wipe it over with a solution of 15g salt, 15ml white vinegar and 250ml hot water (preferably distilled). Rinse immediately and wipe dry.

If verdigris (a green deposit) has developed, wipe over with ammonia, rinse and dry. Alternatively, soak in a warm solution of washing soda for several hours or use a proprietary verdigris remover.

---

**Lacquer**

Lacquering is suitable for both brass and copper. To apply, first make sure the metal is thoroughly clean and has the level of shine you like. Apply a transparent metal lacquer either with a soft brush (do two coats to make sure you do not miss a patch) or with a spray (in which case make sure the surrounding area is protected). From time to time, or if the lacquer becomes damaged, you will need to remove it with a cellulose thinner and clean the brass or copper before re-applying it.

Although lacquer prevents metals from discolouring, a coating will not last long and so is not worth applying to items that you touch a lot, such as door handles and light switches.

---

Where brass is attached to other surfaces, e.g. a chest of drawers with brass handles, make a template of thin card and fix or hold it around the brass area so that it can be cleaned without coating the surrounding area with metal polish.

Lacquered brass is much easier to clean; you have only to wipe it over.

## Bronze

Bronze is a sensitive metal that can be damaged by the chemicals in some cleaning fluids. Most bronze (except bronze cutlery) is intended to have a dull patina and will look unattractive if over-polished. Brush the surface regularly with a clean, soft brush and use a cotton bud to clean out any crevices. If necessary, wash quickly with a solution of soapy water (stale beer is also recommended by some) and wipe dry. Apply a thin layer of dark brown shoe polish and buff with a chamois leather.

Marks on bronze can be removed with paraffin or turpentine applied on a soft cloth followed by a polish and buff.

**Cutlery** is highly susceptible to staining from food and should be washed as soon as possible after meals, then dried and buffed with a soft cloth. Do not put it in a dishwasher as the detergent will be too strong. Clean once or twice a year with a general metal polish and wash and rinse thoroughly before use.

**Outdoor ornaments** are best left to build up a natural patina since it is impossible to keep them clean and shining.

## Carbon steel

See 'Knives', page 64.

## Cast iron

See 'Cast-iron pans', page 66.

**Chromium**  Chromium is a hard metal usually used as plating. Rust on chromium should be removed with wire wool or a proprietary rust remover. The surface should then be washed (using a neutralising solution if you have used a chemical rust remover), dried and sealed with a thin coat of polyurethane varnish. This will not look perfect but will prevent further rusting.

*Bathroom fittings and taps* should be dried after use. If limescale builds up, soak a cloth in malt vinegar and wrap around the affected areas.

*Cars and bicycles* Chromium should be washed, dried and protected with a heavy wax chrome cleaner at regular intervals.

*Furniture* Chromium should be kept dusted and dry. Rub with a soft cloth to maintain shine and remove marks and smears with a little washing-up liquid or bicarbonate of soda applied on a damp cloth. Dry and buff.

**Copper**  Clean as for brass (see page 124).
*Copper saucepans* See page 66.

**Enamel**  Enamel is found mainly on cookware (see 'Vitreous enamel pans', page 67) and baths (see page 72); some ornamental household items are also enamelled. Wash in detergent and warm water and avoid abrasive cleaners and scourers, as enamel scratches easily. Suitable cleaners to use are those recommended by the Vitreous Enamel Association (see 'Enamelled products' in Addresses section). Its symbol (see left) appears on approved products. Always use a plastic bowl in the sink otherwise heavy pots and pans may chip.

**Gold**  Gold does not tarnish so it needs only an occasional wash in warm soapy water, followed by rinsing and drying. Polish occasionally with a chamois leather to retain the shine. Tarnishing may occur if gold is part of an alloy; if this happens, immerse the item in a weak solution of ammonia.

**Gold leaf** This is used particularly for picture frames, and requires dusting only. If it becomes discoloured, dab it gently with a weak solution of ammonia. Gold-leaf paints can be used to touch up damaged areas but the paint will always stand out clearly from the original.

*Pewter*

Pewter should keep its soft sheen and does not need to be polished in the same way as silver. If **antique** pewter is polished to a high shine it may well lose some of its value.

Wash in soapy water, rinse, dry and buff to maintain a low sheen. Remove smears using methylated spirit on a cotton bud. Use a general metal polish if you want a shine.

Where pewter has corroded, rub with fine steel wool (gauge 0000) dipped in fine machine oil. Wipe dry and polish.

Never do anything other than wash and rinse the inside of pewter **tankards** or **goblets** as the metal absorbs smells permanently. Always rinse them immediately after use.

*Platinum*

See 'Gold and platinum', page 133.

*Sheffield plate*

This consists of copper with a very thin coating of silver and is fairly rare compared with conventional silver. Dust well but polish infrequently and very lightly, or you will rub off the silver coating and expose the copper.

*Silver and silver plate*

There is a wide selection of silver cleaners on the market, formulated for different purposes. For silver and silver-plated cutlery that is used on a regular basis but tends to develop light or medium tarnish, use a silver dip which will remove it quickly so you can just rinse the cutlery under running water and polish it dry. The dips do not work well on heavy tarnishing (although repeated applications may clear it) and should not be used on silver-plated cutlery with worn plating.

For cutlery that is used only infrequently, use a polishing mitt or polishing gloves as necessary. For items which spend most of their time in storage, use a silver polishing cloth that contains a tarnish inhibitor. If tarnishing is medium to heavy go for a silver paste that is applied on a damp sponge. This foams up and is also good for removing tarnish from intricate sections where it can be difficult to polish.

Cutlery needs to be kept dry to prevent tarnish. Do not wrap it in newspaper, brown paper, wool or rubber bands, all of which contain sulphur, which produces tarnish. You can buy special bags made from treated fabric for holding cutlery. Acid-free tissue paper also works well.

If silver plating is damaged – and the item is not valuable – you can restore its shine with a silver-coating solution, which you either paint on or immerse the item in. It adds particles of silver to the surface and much improves the appearance. It is less suited to use on cutlery than on articles such as candlesticks and bowls.

---

Always clean silver before storing it. Once clean, keep in tarnish-proof bags or cutlery rolls (see 'Silver storage' in Addresses section)

---

***Stainless steel*** This is a tough metal, although it is stained easily by mineral salts in water so should always be dried immediately after washing; a dishwasher will do this automatically. Polish occasionally with a proprietary product.

*Stainless steel saucepans* See page 67.

## Ornamental materials

Ornamental materials are, in general, not handled very much, so regular light dusting should prevent the need for frequent specific cleaning.

*Alabaster* is porous and should never be washed. Dip a chamois leather in a solution of washing-up liquid and wring out well. Treat stains with cotton wool dipped in turpentine, then buff with a dry chamois leather.

*Alabaster*

Do not put fresh flowers in an alabaster vase. Since the material is porous, the water will leach into it and eventually leak, ruining the appearance of the alabaster. Save the vase for dried, paper or silk flowers.

Bone should not be washed. Wipe over with methylated spirit on cotton wool. Polish any marks with a paste made from whiting (available from good art shops) and methylated spirit applied on a cotton bud. Bone which is very discoloured can be bleached with a paste made from 20-vol hydrogen peroxide and whiting; do not attempt this on anything valuable. See also 'Knives', page 64.

*Bone*

This is usually found on small boxes and oriental ornaments, and consists of coloured enamels painted into a wire frame. Never use water or polish, as it could get into the cracks and damage the enamel. Polish gently with an impregnated silver polishing cloth or simply dust carefully.

*Cloisonné*

**Ebony**  Never use water on ebony as this may damage it. Dust regularly, rubbing well when all dust is removed to retain shine. Very occasionally, apply a little furniture cream.

**Ivory**  The bleaching effect of sunlight is good for ivory but too much sunlight can cause cracking. Extreme cold can cause cracking too, so never leave, say, an ivory-backed hairbrush on a windowsill. Never place ivory in water as this can also cause cracking. Dust ivory regularly with a soft cloth using a clean, soft toothbrush to reach into any carved areas. Wipe over pieces that are not particularly valuable (mirrors and hairbrushes) with methylated spirit applied on cotton wool. Avoid getting perfume or hairspray on ivory as they can cause discoloration.

When washing the bristles of an ivory hairbrush take care not to wet the ivory. Whisk the bristles in a warm soapflake solution, then in clear water. Tap the bristles on a clean white towel to remove as much water as possible and leave to dry naturally, bristles down and away from any heat source.

Valuable antique ivory should be dusted regularly and cleaned professionally if it becomes severely discoloured. See also 'Pianos', page 117.

**Mother-of-pearl**  If mother-of-pearl has lost its lustre through incorrect cleaning, take it to a cutler's or jeweller's for professional cleaning.

*Cutlery handles*  See 'Knives', page 64.

*Inlays*  These are usually found on tabletops and ornamental boxes. Clean the mother-of-pearl with a white furniture cream applied on a cloth or cotton bud. Take care not to touch other parts of the item if they are to be cleaned with another product. Otherwise use furniture cream over the whole surface.

**Ornaments** can be cleaned by making up a paste using powdered whiting (available from good art shops) and warm water. Apply with a soft cloth, then wash briefly in warm soapy water and rinse in warm water. Buff gently.

**Onyx**

Onyx is a porous substance which can even absorb sweat from hands. Hold it in a duster while you dust it with another. Remove light marks with cotton wool moistened in methylated spirit. Onyx table surfaces will absorb anything spilled on them, so wipe immediately. If liquid is absorbed, the onyx will need to be reground professionally to get rid of the mark and then re-polished.

**Ormolu**

Ormolu consists of gold leaf overlaid on bronze and is found on decorated furniture. Apply a solution of 10ml ammonia in a cup of warm water on a cotton bud, taking care not to spill any on surrounding wood. Make a cardboard template for larger areas. Rinse with clear water on a cotton wool ball and dry with a soft cloth. Do not use metal polish as this will damage the finish.

**Soapstone**

Clean as for bone (see page 129).

## Jewellery

Both 'real' and costume jewellery need care in cleaning. Check valuable and antique jewellery carefully: if stones are loose or claws broken, get them repaired by a jeweller. It is a good idea to have any valuable items checked and cleaned professionally once a year as a jeweller may detect weak spots that you haven't noticed. In addition, professional cleaning produces a shine that is hard to achieve at home. You could combine the cleaning with a revaluation of your jewellery for insurance purposes.

Another option is to invest in a jewellery cleaning machine that works using sonic rays. These are fairly expensive so unless you own a large amount of jewellery and need to clean it on a regular basis it is more economical to use the methods described below.

Do not use a chemical jewellery cleaner on costume jewellery unless you are sure that it will not discolour or lose its lacquer. Imitation gold and silver are best washed and dried.

---

**Washing jewellery**

- Use a plastic bowl filled with warm water and a little washing-up liquid. Never wash jewellery in a sink; if the plug becomes dislodged your jewellery may disappear down the drain.

- Place the jewellery in the washing solution, making sure that the items are not touching each other, and soak for a few minutes.

- Remove each piece individually and brush it gently with an old soft toothbrush (or a baby's toothbrush kept specifically for cleaning). If dirt or soap are difficult to get at, use a cocktail stick or toothpick to ease it out gently.

- Rinse the items well and place them on a clean linen tea-towel (not a fluffy one) to dry. Use the cool setting of a fan-heater or hair-dryer to speed up the process.

- Return the jewellery to its storage case, box or carrying roll. Do not leave pieces jumbled together in a drawer or they may become damaged. Diamonds, for example, can cut other stones and chains may become entangled. (If this happens, dust the chains lightly with talcum powder and use a sewing needle to disentangle them or remove the knots.)

- Before discarding the washing solution, drain it through a sieve to check that no stone, bead or earring has been overlooked.

---

These include **amber, coral** and **jet**, and can be washed following the method described opposite. Never put fragile stones into a chemical solution. **Cameos** need special treatment and should not be washed or immersed in anything but cleaned with a soft brush dipped in a jewellery-cleaning solution.

*Fragile stones*

These include **amethysts, diamonds, rubies** and **sapphires**, and can be cleaned using the treatment described opposite or a chemical jewellery-cleaning solution. Another effective treatment is to soak them in a solution of cold water and household ammonia in equal parts, then drain on kitchen paper.

*Hard stones*

Emeralds are softer than other precious stones and chip easily. If you wash stones which are cracked, water will seep in and make any flaws visible. It is best to have emeralds cleaned professionally and to restrict home care to polishing with a clean, dry chamois leather.

*Emeralds*

These metal items may gather dirt for a long time before you actually notice it. Immerse them in methylated spirit for a couple of minutes, then rinse and dry well. Polish with a chamois leather.

*Gold and platinum*

A gentle wipe with a soft cloth should keep jade clean – washing is generally unnecessary unless it is handled a lot. If you do wash jade, dry it immediately with a soft cloth or paper towel. Make sure that any cloth you use is free from grit as jade has a soft surface which scratches easily.

*Jade*

This should not be washed. Rub it over with a soft, dry toothbrush and polish with a chamois leather.

*Marcasite*

**Opals and turquoise** These should never be washed. Rub them over with a chamois leather and use a soft toothbrush to clean any claw settings.

**Pearls** These should never be washed as oils from the skin improve their sheen; the more you wear them the more they shine. If you wear them infrequently rub them gently with a chamois leather from time to time. Always apply hair-spray, make-up or scent *before* putting on pearls, as these can damage their appearance.

**Silver** Use a silver dip if you are in a hurry; no deposits from the dip will settle in the cracks. A better finish will be obtained with a silver polish, or by gently rubbing the item with a soft brush coated with toothpaste, then rinsing off. Solid silver items such as chunky bracelets are best cleaned with a long-term silver polish.

---

**Protecting jewellery during housework**
- Do not let set stones come into contact with household bleach while you are cleaning, as bleach may damage the metal mounts.
- Use a safety-pin to clip rings to your lapel or apron when you are cleaning or cooking.
- Do not wear jewellery while doing any rough work, such as DIY or gardening. A hard knock can damage even the toughest stone.

---

## Personal items

For hygiene reasons, it is particularly important to keep items for personal wear scrupulously clean. This applies particularly to contact lenses and dentures.

**Contact lenses** Use the special cleaner and fluids recommended by your optician. Do not use spittle – particularly with soft lenses – as it can cause infection. Never sleep with your lenses in, unless they are specifically designed for this, as this makes them harder to clean and is not good for your eyes.

Contact-lens-cleaning solutions are expensive, not because of their ingredients but because you are paying for the strict hygiene conditions under which they are produced. Always keep containers closed when not in use, put them in a cool place and observe the date after which they should be thrown out.

## Dentures

While you can buy a range of denture cleaners and follow the instructions, it is equally easy – and cheaper – to use soap and water. Fill a washbasin with tepid (not hot) water and use a nailbrush and soap. Never use toothpaste as it will abrade the pink plastic and remove its high gloss. Also the scratching will make cleaning more difficult. The reason for filling the washbasin is that the dentures become slippery as you clean and if you accidentally drop them they will float instead of breaking on a hard surface. To clean upper dentures, use an up-and-down movement on the teeth and scrub carefully in between the areas that touch the outside cheek and palate and the gums.

Clean lower dentures in the same way but avoid holding them in the palm of your hand, which may squeeze and snap the horseshoe. Dentures are fragile when not held in place by the jaw. Hold one side at a time as you work.

Clean dentures twice a day, otherwise calcium and tartar from the saliva will build up and you will need to pay for professional cleaning by a dentist.

## Spectacles

It is important to clean spectacles regularly as a build-up of dirt interferes with the way light travels through the lenses. Special cloths, available from opticians, literally slice off the dirt. They are made from a special fibre which is long-lasting and washable.

To clean spectacles thoroughly, rinse them under cold or tepid running water, then in a solution of washing-up liquid. Rinse and wipe with a soft, non-fluffy cloth. Do not use paper tissues as some brands contain particles of wood pulp which can scratch the lenses.

Many opticians will clean your spectacles free of charge using an autosonic system, which gets out the dirt that lodges between the lens and the frame.

If you have a greasy build-up on lenses you can use surgical or methylated spirit, but take care not to get these chemicals on plastic frames or enamelled metal or on the skin of your face.

## Wigs and hairpieces

Synthetic wigs should be cleaned in a solution of washing-up liquid or laundry detergent and left to dry naturally. Modern wigs do not melt under a hair-dryer (use the cool setting), but natural drying is recommended.

Machine-made human hair wigs should be cleaned with shampoo for normal hair, followed by conditioner (essential, since natural oils from the head do not get into the hair). You can use a dryer to style them.

Hand-knotted human hair wigs need to be cleaned with a special dry-cleaning fluid that is not available over the counter; you therefore need to use a specialist wig cleaner (see 'Wigs' in Addresses section).

Wigs supplied on the National Health Service are usually synthetic and are cleaned free of charge (two wigs are supplied to those who need them); extra cleaning must be paid for. If you buy your own wig it will probably be human hair, which tends to move when wet so must be blocked into position the minute shampooing is over or it will lose its style. Do not use a polystyrene wig stand for this (although it is perfectly all right for normal off-the-head storage) but buy a cork and linen stand (see 'Wigs' in Addresses section), which will support the wig while drying naturally.

## Leisure and hobby items

It is easy to neglect the cleaning of items you use for leisure. However, cleaning is essential for the maintenance of anything that contains mechanical parts; and for other items, you could be surprised by the improvement that it makes to them.

***Binoculars and telescopes***

Clean only on the outside. Consult a photographic dealer or other specialist if there is dirt inside. Wipe over the casing with a clean soft cloth after use. Clean the outside of lenses by dusting with a lint-free cloth, then with a cloth impregnated with a special lens-cleaning fluid (available from photographic dealers).

***Cameras***

Unless you are an expert photographer and fully conversant with your photographic equipment it is best to leave its cleaning to an expert. Your local camera shop may be able to do it or should be able to put you in touch with someone who can.

***Card tables***

Keep the folding-leg mechanism lubricated with a general-purpose aerosol. Brush the baize surface or use the upholstery tool of your vacuum cleaner. If drinks are spilled, mop up immediately and treat as for the relevant stain (see Chapter 2, Stain removal). Using a cloth when playing will help to protect the baize; velvet is best for the easy sliding of cards.

> Clean dirty playing cards by rubbing with white, crustless bread

**Embroidery** See 'Embroidered covers', page 95.

**Pianos** See page 117.

**Portable radios** These tend to collect dust on plastic surfaces, particularly if used in the kitchen, where grease particles contribute to dirt build-up. Dust regularly with a feather or fluffy duster brush and from time to time use a cotton bud dipped in methylated spirit to clear grime from around knobs and dials.

**Records and CDs** Use a specialist cleaning pack, available from record shops. Brush records (but not discs) before and after every use with a soft brush or velvet cleaning pad. Always put records back in their sleeves after use. CDs are less easily damaged than vinyl records but are best stored in their cases.

**Sewing machines** Clean the casing with a spray cleaner/polish, making sure that it is rubbed in well and will not get on to any fabric being sewn.

Use the brush supplied with the sewing machine (or buy one from a supplier) to brush out the residue of fabric 'lint' that collects underneath the bobbin.

Clean the machine every time you use it to prevent a build-up of lint.

**Televisions and videos** Clean the television cabinet with a product suitable for the material it is made from. If plastic, use an anti-static spray to prevent it attracting dust. Keep the screen clean by spraying window-cleaner over it once a week and buffing with a paper towel. It is also worth investing in anti-static disposable wipes for cleaning (see Chapter 9, 'Products that work').

Cover your video recorder when it is not in use to prevent dust getting in the vents. Avoid standing drinks on top of it, which, besides staining the top, could spill and damage the works. If something does spill, wipe immediately with a damp cloth. Otherwise, do not use liquid cleaning products on your video recorder – just dust regularly. Silica gel sachets (from electrical retailers) should be put on top of the video recorder if the room is prone to condensation.

**Toys** Clean non-washable toys by putting them in a plastic bag filled with bicarbonate of soda and shaking thoroughly. Brush off the powder out of doors.

## Office equipment

Many homes now have at least one item of what was once regarded as 'office' equipment. But while items in an office are often maintained under service contracts, in your home they are your responsibility, and failure to keep them clean may result in expensive call-out charges for professional cleaning and repair.

When you buy a piece of equipment it should come with care instructions, perhaps even with specialised cleaning tools. Always follow the instructions carefully and try to clean the equipment once a week.

**Computers** *Screen* Dust before each use. Always use lint-free cloths or anti-static wipes (see Chapter 9, Products that work). A little anti-static spray will help to keep dust at bay. Even better, use a monitor cover. Clean the outside of the machine by dusting and remove any marks with a damp cloth or methylated spirit. An aerosol cleaner or polish should be applied occasionally. *Keyboard* This should be cleaned with methylated spirit applied on a cotton bud.

Keep the screen and keyboard covered when not in use. When using the machine, keep drinks and cigarette ash at arm's length.

> Always switch off electrical equipment before cleaning.

**Printers**  Wipe over the exterior with a duster or anti-static cloth when dust builds up but leave the inside well alone. Provided you keep it closed, and possibly covered, dirt should not be a problem. Regular servicing will prevent the printer malfunctioning due to dust or grit inside it.

**Photocopiers**  For correction fluid spills, see page 29. For all other cleaning or maintenance, consult the manufacturer – DIY is not recommended.

**Typewriters**  New typewriters usually come supplied with a cleaning kit consisting of brushes and cleaning fluid. Use the brush supplied or a small synthetic fluffy brush to remove dust. Use methylated spirit applied on a cotton bud to clean the keys and in between them. Check the inside of the machine once a week and use methylated spirit on a cotton bud to remove any ink stains.

If you use your typewriter a lot, have it serviced and cleaned professionally once a year. Keep covered when not in use.

**Telephones and mobile phones**  Clean telephones as for fax machines (opposite). If your telephone has a dial, use a cotton bud dipped in methylated spirit to reach behind it. All phones, including mobiles, should be cleaned frequently as germs can build up on them and can spread, particularly if used by more than one person. Telephone cleaner wipes that are impregnated with a bacteria-killing solution should be used daily to reduce the risk of ear and mouth infections. Alternatively, wipe the ear- and mouthpieces with a little antiseptic fluid applied on cotton wool.

Dust with a small, fluffy, synthetic brush. Rub the brush between your hands before use – this will create static, which will pick up dust effectively. Use methylated spirit to clean off any marks and wipe the keypad with a cotton bud dipped in methylated spirit to keep the keys clean.

*Fax machines*

Dust with a synthetic fluffy brush. Apply a small amount of aerosol cleaner or polish on a soft clean cloth. Remove the tape(s) at intervals and dust the inside of the machine, either with a small battery-run vacuum cleaner or a damp cloth. Make sure the interior is dry before replacing the tapes.

*Answering machines*

# Chapter 5

# Care of clothes, shoes and bags

Laundry

Dry-cleaning

Clothes

Sportswear

Shoes and bags

## Laundry

Laundry is one cleaning task that cannot be escaped. There is a huge range of products on the market, ranging from own-brands to esoteric; cheap to expensive; in the form of powder, liquid or gel capsules. It is worth trying a selection to see what best meets your needs.

***Getting good results from washing*** Use the specified amount of detergent for both machine- and hand-washing. If you use too little the garments will not be clean; using too much is wasteful.

Do not mix strong colours with white and pastel colours as the lighter colours will eventually develop a greyish tinge and may pick up loose colour from the stronger dyes. If this happens, use a dye-removal product that takes out colour.

Do not leave wet washing in the machine, where it may develop mildew. Tumble-dry or hang out somewhere airy. For the same reason, always wash and dry wet swimming costumes or rain-sodden clothes as soon as you can.

---

**Loading the washing-machine**
- Do not overload. The chart on page 150 shows how much items of clothing weigh. Make sure you do not overload the half-load program either.
- Try to mix large and small items in one load. If you just wash large items such as sheets, they tend to wrap around each other.
- Wash delicate items, which might snag, inside a pillow case or purpose-made net bag (see 'Textiles' in Addresses section).

---

***Before washing*** Check garments before you wash them. Do up zips and fastenings. Empty all pockets – coins can damage the machine, tissues will shred all over the wash-load, and bank notes will take time and effort to replace!

*Soaking* If an item is very dirty, soak it first. Unless you have a large sink the bath is the best place for this. Make sure that the powder or liquid you use is fully dissolved *before* you soak the garment and that it is completely immersed. You may need to weigh down the item with something, such as a bathrack.

> If black clothes have faded it will usually be due to a build-up of soap. Unless the garment is dry-clean-only, soak in warm water with a little vinegar added to restore to former glory.

If you are using a biological powder, check the packet to see whether it is suitable for use on the fabric. Soak for half an hour or so in lukewarm water or overnight in cold water. For a cold-water soak first dissolve the powder in a jug or bowl of hot water, then mix it into the cold water.

> Soak dirty handkerchiefs overnight in salt water before washing, to loosen mucus.

> **Washing powder**
> You will probably need more than one type of washing powder. The following should be sufficient for most people's needs:
>
> - washing-machine powder or detergent suitable for coloured fabrics
> - hand-washing powder or detergent containing bleach for white items
> - biological soaking powder.
>
> For dirty sports clothes or dirty work overalls you may need a heavier-duty product than would be necessary for ordinary dirty washing.

*Fabric conditioner* This is used in addition to a washing product and reduces dirt-attracting static and creasing. However, after a time it can decrease the absorbency of towels. It makes ironing easier, particularly if you fold clothes carefully when they are dry. Fabric conditioner is available in two forms: as a liquid which goes in one of the detergent-dispensing drawers of the washing-machine and which is added to the last rinse, or as impregnated papers which are put into the tumble-dryer.

> Always wash garments with a textured finish inside-out as the texture may be damaged by rubbing against other items.

**Hand-washing** Hand-washing is recommended for items that cannot take the very hot water and high agitation levels of a washing-machine.

You may also prefer to hand-wash some items that are recommended for machine-washing, particularly if you think the colour might run.

> **Checking for colour fastness**
> • Dampen a section of the item with water.
> • Place a piece of white cotton rag or an old white handkerchief on top of the section and press down with an iron on the cool setting.
> • If colour comes off on the handkerchief, the fabric is likely to run.
> • Some colours run more than others. Red and deep-blue dyes are notorious.

Use soapflakes or a detergent specially formulated for hand-washing, making sure that the solution is completely dissolved before you put the clothes in. The best method is to dissolve the powder in a small bowl of hot water, then add this to the main wash water.

Although it is always sensible to wear household gloves when hand-washing, check the temperature of the water before you put them on – it is difficult to judge this correctly with gloves on.

---

**White socks**

Put 30ml bicarbonate of soda in the washing water and a squirt of lemon juice in the rinse water for really good results.

---

Save the unusable ends of bars of soap and use them instead of soapflakes when hand-washing.

---

*Rinsing* Do not skimp on rinsing. A washing-machine rinses several times and so must you. With some garments you can use the rinse and spin program of a washing-machine to remove water, although a spin-dryer is easier to control. If you have neither, squeeze the garment gently, placing delicate fabrics in a towel to absorb water.

Check whether items can be tumble-dried. If not, dry on a line or indoor airer. Sweaters should be pulled into shape and dried flat on a net frame (available from hardware shops) placed over the bath or in the garden.

The chart on page 151 shows what the international washing care symbols mean. If you are making up a mixed load for the washing-machine you should program it to wash at the lowest temperature given on a care label even if the other items can stand hotter water. However, to be really clean, fabrics need to be

*Understanding care labels*

washed at the recommended temperature every third or fourth time. The half-load facility which all modern machines have can be useful for this purpose.

**Laundering household linen**

Towels, bath mats, tablecloths and mats, napkins and tea towels should all be laundered according to the instructions on the care label.

Keep fluffy and non-fluffy items in separate loads, or fluff may transfer.

Rinse tea towels in a weak starch solution after washing. This prevents them shedding fluff when drying china and glass.

Starching may sound old-fashioned but it does improve the appearance of cottons and linens and makes table linen look good for special occasions. Choose from traditional powder, instant powder or spray starch and follow the instructions. You can also buy a starching dip which is quick and easy to use. Remember to clean the iron after starching (see page 64).

---

**Sterilising tea-towels**

Ironing tea-towels has a sterilising effect – useful if you have laundered them at a low temperature in a mixed wash.

---

**Detergent build-up on towels**

Detergents can build up on towels, producing a whitish bloom on coloured fabrics. If this happens, machine-wash using the same amount of water-softening powder as you would detergent.

---

**Laundering nappies**

To prevent terry towelling nappies becoming heavily soiled, use disposable nappy liners inside them. These can be safely flushed down the lavatory.

Soak wet or soiled nappies in a proprietary nappy-soaking solution as soon as you take them off the baby, and leave them there until you are ready to wash them. Take care to mix the solution according to the manufacturer's instructions. Nappies can be damaged if the solution is too strong as it contains a quantity of bleach.

Wash nappies at 95–100°C to clean and sterilise them. Keep an eye out for any irritation on the baby, such as a rash or soreness; some babies cannot tolerate biological washing powders.

Tumble-dry nappies and stack ready-folded to put on the baby.

## Dry-cleaning

This is an essential cleaning process for items that cannot be washed. You may find that you buy a garment with a dry-clean-only label which you think you should be able to wash; this is a precaution used by some manufacturers who are concerned about dye running and shrinkage.

*General care tips*

If you do decide to wash an item that is labelled 'dry-clean only', wash separately by hand. This is not recommended for anything expensive or that you treasure, but may save you money on, say, a dry-clean-only T-shirt.

Use a dry-cleaner which is a member of the Textile Services Association (see 'Textiles in Addresses section). This organisation operates a code of practice and runs an arbitration service to help resolve disputes when things go wrong.

Note that dry-cleaning symbols sometimes specify a particular solvent (see chart on page 151); check that the dry-cleaner you intend to use has access to it. One dry-cleaning chemical called fluorocarbon has been phased out for

## Washing weights for laundry

| Garment | Fabric type | Weight |
|---|---|---|
| Denim jeans | cotton | 700g (1lb 8oz) |
| Dress | cotton<br>synthetic mix | 500g (1lb 2oz)<br>350g (12 oz) |
| Man's shirt | cotton/synthetic mix | 200g (7oz) |
| Nappies (10) | terry towelling | 1kg (2lb 3oz) |
| Socks (1 pair) | cotton/synthetic mix | 50g (2oz) |
| T-shirt | cotton | 100g (4oz) |
| Underwear (per item) | cotton/synthetic mix | 50g (2oz) |
| Woman's blouse/shirt | cotton<br>synthetic mix | 150g (5oz)<br>100g (4oz) |

### Household linen

| Garment | Fabric type | Weight |
|---|---|---|
| Bath towel | cotton/synthetic mix | 700g (1lb 8oz) |
| Duvet cover (double) | synthetic mix | 1kg (2lb 3oz) |
| Duvet cover (single) | synthetic mix | 700g (1lb 8oz) |
| Pillow case | cotton/synthetic mix | 150g (5oz) |
| Sheet (double) | cotton/synthetic mix | 500g (1lb 2oz) |
| Sheet (single) | cotton/synthetic mix | 450g (1lb) |
| Tablecloth (large) | cotton/synthetic mix/plastic | 700g (1lb 8oz) |
| Tablecloth (small) | cotton/synthetic mix | 250g (9oz) |
| Tea-towel | cotton/linen | 100g (4oz) |

**Note** It is important not to overload your washing-machine, so use this list as a guide to making up a load. Clothes will get cleaner if they can move freely within the drum, so do not load the machine up to the maximum weight if it already appears full.

To weigh your own wash-load, put everything into a pillow case or a plastic carrier-bag. Either balance it on your bathroom scales or stand on them yourself, first with the bag and then without it. Subtract the difference.

## Care symbols

| | Words on label | Washing temperature | |
|---|---|---|---|
| | | machine | hand |
| ⊔95 | wash in cotton cycle/program *or* wash as cotton | very hot 95°C *normal action, rinse and spin* | hand hot 50°C |
| ⊔60 | wash in cotton cycle/program *or* wash as cotton | hot 60°C | hand hot 50°C |
| ⊔50 | wash in synthetics cycle/program *or* wash as synthetics | hand hot 50°C *reduced action, cold rinse, reduced spin or drip dry* | see care label |
| ⊔40 | wash in cotton cycle/program *or* wash as cotton | warm 40°C *normal action, rinse and spin* | see care label |
| ⊔40 | wash in synthetics cycle/program *or* wash as synthetics | warm 40°C *reduced action, cold rinse, reduced spin* | see care label |
| ⊔40 | wash in wool cycle/program *or* wash as wool | warm 40°C *much reduced action, normal rinse* | see care label |
| ⊔ | hand-wash | see care label | |
| ⊠ | do not wash | | |

△CI    may be chlorine-bleached

⊠    do not chlorine-bleach

◯    tumble-dry

⊠    do not tumble-dry

🖶    hot iron (cotton, linen, viscose)

🖶    warm iron (polyester mixtures, wool)

🖶    cool iron (acetate, acrylic, nylon, polyester, triacetate)

⊠    do not iron

Ⓐ    dry-clean (in any solvents)

Ⓟ    Ⓟ    dry-clean (suitable for dry-cleaning with perchlorethylene, a chemical with high solvency power which is used in a particular type of machine. Seek the advice of a specialist dry-cleaning firm).

Ⓕ    Ⓕ    dry-clean in fluorocarbon. This chemical has been phased out. It should be possible to clean garments marked Ⓕ as in Ⓟ above. Good dry-cleaners will know how to moderate the solution to suit particular fabrics.

⊗    do not dry-clean

environmental reasons. Garments marked with F (see chart) may be cleaned in perchlorethylene: good dry-cleaners will know how to moderate the solution for the correct result on a particular fabric.

> All dry cleaning chemicals are, to a greater or lesser degree, toxic. It is important to air garments thoroughly after dry-cleaning to make sure all the residual fumes have dissipated.

For very valuable or treasured items you may want to use a guaranteed high-quality cleaner which accepts items by post. Check in advance what the cost will be, and also that items are insured while in transit.

A cleaner which specialises in cleaning theatrical costumes is a good bet, as these have to last and are often made from complex fabrics and trimmings.

Coin-operated dry-cleaning can be a bit hit-and-miss. If the outlet is completely unattended it is probably best to go elsewhere. The quality of the result will very much depend on how often the solvent in the machines is changed. Check this and try to be first in the queue when it has just been changed. Also check that the solvent used is suitable for the item you are cleaning. Most coin-operated dry-cleaners use a basic chemical and you may find your care label specifies something else.

*Items that should be dry-cleaned*

- Tailored clothing that will lose its shape if washed.
- Jersey wool (unless labelled as washable).
- Items with a special finish.
- Anything made from more than one fabric: washing may cause one fabric to shrink or lose colour at a different rate from the other.

---

**Ways to cut your dry-cleaning bills**

Dry cleaning is expensive but with a little time and trouble you can cut down on the frequency.

- Follow the general care advice (below) – brushing your clothes when you take them off, airing them and hanging them properly will reduce the need for frequent cleaning.
- Press garments that are not actually dirty but are beginning to look in need of a good clean.
- Use an aerosol dry-cleaning product on grubby collars and cuffs.

## Clothes

Clothes repay care. If you look after them correctly they will continue to look good for longer. Fortunately, care labels are now stitched into every new garment.

Some garments require special care if they are to maintain their shape and colour. Refer to the advice on specific materials in this section if you are in any doubt.

***General care tips***

- When you take off your clothes at the end of the day, check for any problems such as stains, loose threads and missing buttons.
- If the clothes you have been wearing do not need washing, they will benefit from an airing before you put them away. Clothes tend to pick up smells – from outside sources as well as from your body. These will disperse more quickly in an open room than in a cupboard or chest of drawers.
- Hang or fold clothes carefully when not in use.
- Brush garments (particularly coats and suits) when you take them off. If they are wet allow to dry before brushing.
- Treat stains as soon as they occur. (See Chapter 2, Stain removal, for specific treatments.)

- Shiny patches on clothes can be remedied by wiping with a cloth dipped in 10ml white vinegar in 250ml water.
- Remove any fluff or pilling that may have developed, either with a clothes-brush or by wrapping sticky tape round a finger and dabbing the affected area. Electrical devices to remove pilling are available but they tend to remove body from the fabric.

---

**Storing clothes**
- Clothes that are to be stored for some time – summer or winter garments, for example – should be cleaned first. Do not bother to iron things before you store them; you will only have to iron them again when you take them out. Avoid using fabric conditioner on clothes that are to be stored as this can accelerate mould growth.
- Make sure that the place where you store clothes is dry and use a herbal or chemical moth-repellent.

---

If your clothes are crushed and you do not have access to an iron, hang them in a steamy bathroom and the creases should drop out.

---

**Acetate**  Hand- or machine-wash at a low temperature and do not wring. Iron while still damp.

**Acrylic**  Most acrylic garments can be machine-washed but always check the care label. **Acrylic jumpers** should be pulled into shape after washing and dried flat.

Angora should be hand-washed in cool water. **Angora**
When dry use a teasel brush to raise the fluff.

Wash or dry-clean according to the fabric. Iron **Brocade**
gently so as not to flatten the brocade. **Velvet
brocade** should be dry-cleaned by a specialist.

Wash or dry-clean according to the fabric. Iron **Broderie**
gently, taking care not to enlarge the holes. If **anglaise**
you are washing broderie anglaise together with
items which have zips or hooks and eyes,
enclose it in a pillow case.

This should be dry-cleaned as washing makes it **Buckram**
go floppy. It is important to check whether your
curtain headings contain buckram: if they do
they must be dry-cleaned, regardless of the fabric of the curtains themselves.

Scrub with a stiff nailbrush and unperfumed **Canvas**
soap. Rinse thoroughly.

Hand-wash in cool water using soapflakes or a **Cashmere**
specialist hand-washing product. Some cash-
mere can be machine-washed on delicates.
Press inside-out with a cool iron.

Cheesecloth can be machine-washed and does **Cheesecloth**
not need ironing – simply pull into shape.

Chiffon should be hand-washed at a low tem- **Chiffon**
perature and ironed on a cool setting while
damp. Valuable items should be dry-cleaned.

Wash inside-out according to care label. Iron **Corduroy**
inside-out while damp. Smooth the pile into the
right direction with a soft cloth while drying.

Denim will shrink unless already pre-shrunk, as **Denim**
is the norm. Check the care label carefully.

Wash separately until you are sure there is no colour run. Iron while very damp.

**Jeans** should be washed inside-out to avoid streaky lines on the denim.

*Fur*    Fur needs to be dry-cleaned. If fur gets wet, allow to dry naturally on a hanger in a draught away from direct heat.

Never store fur in plastic; always use a cotton or silk bag and hang on a well-padded hanger. Valuable furs will remain in better condition if put into cold storage during the warm months of the year.

Furs which are not worn regularly should be shaken from time to time.

For **imitation fur**, follow the care label instructions. Some types can be washed; others need dry-cleaning.

> If you wear a fur coat it will need professional cleaning from time to time. For home treatment, beat with a bamboo cane then use a stiff brush on it. Always shake the coat before you put it on and take care not to sit so that an area becomes rubbed.

*Hats*    Clean hats according to the material they are made from. Marks on **velour** and **velvet** should be treated with a grease solvent, then held in the steam from a boiling kettle. Stuff with paper to keep the shape when stored. **Straw** hats should be brushed to remove dust.

*Lace*    Valuable or antique lace should be given specialist care (see 'Textiles' in Addresses section). Otherwise, hand-wash in a mild detergent – one that does not contain bleach, which would rot it. If you have removed lace from a garment to wash it separately, make a template of the shape before washing so you can pull it back to the correct shape. Treat any stains before washing.

Dry flat on a white towel or jumper-drying rack; do not place in direct sunlight, which can cause it to yellow. Do not press unless essential, in which case cover the ironing-board with a white towel, put the lace face-downwards, cover with a cloth and press with a cool iron.

**Leather and suede**

Many leathers and suedes are genuinely washable, although some should only be sponged or dry-cleaned. Look carefully at the care label when you buy a leather garment. Leather or suede with a dull finish is easily stained, so use a spray protector at home or ask a dry-cleaner to do it for you. Always test first in an inconspicuous area to make sure there is no colour change.

To keep suede looking good you need to rub over it gently with a suede brush or another piece of suede.

Most leather and suede will need to be dry-cleaned occasionally. This always results in colour change, so make sure that, for example, you take all parts of a suit at the same time.

> After washing leather gloves, put them on while still damp, for about ten minutes, to prevent shrinkage and ensure they stay in shape.

**Linen**

Test coloured linens for colour fastness (see page 146). Wash according to the care label. Iron while still quite damp.

**Mohair**

Wash as for angora (page 155).

**Muslin**

Wash at high temperature. Stretch into shape while still damp.

**Satin**  Wash according to the care label. Dry-clean upholstery satin.

**Seersucker**  Wash according to the fibre and drip-dry. Do not iron, or you will flatten the finish.

**Silk**  Most silk garments can now be machine-washed; otherwise hand-wash. Iron while slightly and evenly damp.

**Velvet**  Velvet can usually be machine- or hand-washed according to the care label. Dry-clean if you are concerned about colour run or damage.

**Viscose**  Viscose can be washed by hand or at low machine temperature. Stretch into shape while damp.

**Viyella**  Machine-wash on a delicates program. Use a cool iron while damp.

---

### Caring for clothes while travelling

- Carry a small clothes-brush or fluff-removing gadget with you. Often, all that is needed for a garment that is looking soiled is a good going-over to remove dust, débris, dandruff and so on.
- When you take off a garment do a quick spot-check to see whether it needs attention. Collars and cuffs may benefit from a brush and sponge over with lukewarm water; muddy hems should be left to dry, brushed and sponged with warm water.
- If you are away from home and a garment gets stained, go for the soap and water treatment. Use the corner of a white towel and a little soap and water to attack whatever has been spilled.
- Carry a small tube, stick or bottle of all-purpose grease solvent in your handbag, sponge bag, pocket or luggage.

These should be brushed well when dirty. Re-waterproofing products are available should you need them (check with the manufacturer). **_Waterproofed fabrics_**

If the item is not machine-washable, wash by hand. When hand-washing woollens, it is sensible to draw the outline of the garment on a piece of white card or paper before washing. In this way you can stretch the item to its correct shape and size when drying. If you do not want crease marks along the sleeves of jumpers, put an inner tube from clingfilm or kitchen foil into the sleeves, covering the tube with clingfilm first so that the cardboard does not mark the wool. **_Wool_**

## Sportswear

Specialised sportswear may require the particular cleaning treatments outlined below. For activities such as running or working out, comfortable and loose clothing, such as T-shirt and shorts, is usually worn. Since these tend to get very sweaty, soak in biological detergent before washing unless this is precluded by the packet instructions. If it is, use the heavy dirt cycle on the washing machine.

See page 180. **_Camping gear_**

Grass stains tend to be the main problem. Dab with methylated spirit (but not on acetates and triacetates) and rinse before laundering. If the flannels are dry-clean only, cover the stain with an equal mixture of salt and cream of tartar and leave for 15 minutes. Brush off and repeat if the stain remains. **_Cricket flannels_**

Brush to remove surface soil, then treat with a product designed to clean canvas shoes. **_Cricket pads_**

If a cricket sweater starts to look grey, soak in a solution of proprietary water softener powder diluted according to the manufacturer's instructions. **_Cricket sweaters_**

159

**Riding macs**   Riding macs cannot normally be washed or dry-cleaned. In the absence of other instructions, scrub with a nailbrush dipped in a mild detergent solution, taking care to overlap on sections cleaned so that lines do not appear. Wipe over with a damp cloth, pat dry with a towel and hang to dry. Do not treat the inside.

**Sailing gear**   Sailing gear should never be left lying around, otherwise it will develop mildew and permanent creases.

*Guernseys* should be hand-washed and rinsed, then placed in a pillow case and spun briefly. Dry over a clothes-line, turning frequently. Do not dry flat as the close knit means it will take a long time to dry and mildew may develop.

*Heavy wool sweaters* are best hand-washed. Soak in a cold hand-washing solution, then rinse in cold water. Do not rub or wring. Spin briefly in a washing-machine or spin-dryer, then dry flat.

*Oiled-wool sweaters* should be washed as infrequently as possible, as washing removes the oil. Use a warm soapflake solution and rinse in warm water containing 5ml olive oil. Dry flat.

*Oilskins* should not be washed or dry-cleaned but collars and cuffs can be rubbed with neat washing-up liquid, then sponged with clean water.

**Swimming costumes**   Always rinse these in cool, clean water after swimming – whether in a pool or in the sea – and dry immediately. It is particularly important to remove chlorine, salt and any suntan preparations.

The costume should have a care label or have come with instructions for laundering depending on the material it is made from. Follow these, particularly if storing the costume for a while.

Never leave a damp swimming costume in a plastic bag for more than a couple of hours as mildew will develop and the costume will rot.

If you swim a lot you should wash your costume regularly. Most are machine-washable, but you should never wring out or tumble-dry your costume, or place it on a radiator.

See page 162.

**Trainers**

White clothing such as tennis shorts and tops will need an occasional soak in biological detergent to brighten them up.

**Whites**

## Shoes and bags

If possible, when shoes are worn for long periods during the day, do not wear the same pair two days running. When you take them off, leave them out to air for a while before putting them in a cupboard. Bags and luggage (see pages 163–4) are worth keeping clean, as dirt on these can easily rub off on clothes.

Footwear fabrics vary from canvas to satin and should be treated accordingly. Slightly soiled fabrics can be cleaned with a proprietary shampoo suitable for the fabric. Wet the upper with a damp cloth, rub in the shampoo, then wipe over with a damp cloth. Brush when dry. Stuff shoes with newspaper or shoe trees when cleaning and dry at room temperature.

**Fabric shoes**

Colour can be restored with a whitener or coloured shoe-care product.

Some fabric shoes are machine-washable. If this is the case, wash them with towels, otherwise they will make a lot of noise as they spin round the machine.

***Patent leather*** Clean with a soft cloth and polish with an instant shoe-shine pad. When wet, stuff

**Leather and suede shoes**

with newspaper and dry well away from any heat source, which could cause the leather to crack.

**Smooth leather** Remove any mud with a blunt piece of wood or the blunt edge of a knife, then sponge with a damp cloth. Stuff the shoes with newspaper or shoe trees to keep them in shape and allow to dry naturally away from any heat source. When dry, apply polish or shoe cream and allow to dry again, preferably overnight so that the polish can 'feed' the leather. Polish with a clean cloth or soft-bristled brush.

For grease stains on leather shoes, see page 41.

**Suede** Brush off dust regularly and remove mud with a nylon, rubber or soft brass wire suede-brush. Use a damp cloth to get rid of any residue. If the shoes are wet, allow them to dry naturally. Use a proprietary stain remover on oil and grease stains, applying several times if necessary. Check first on an inconspicuous area (e.g. the tongue of the shoe) that it will not leave a tide mark. (See page 48 for treatment of water marks.)

If the nap has been flattened, hold the shoe about 15cm from the spout of a steaming (not boiling) kettle, then brush using a circular motion. Use emery paper or a blunt knife to raise small areas of badly flattened nap.

If the colour has faded, use a proprietary dressing over the whole shoe, going over the paler areas first.

**Riding boots** Treat **leather** riding boots with good-quality leather food. Leave on overnight and buff the next day. Treat scratches with a coloured reno-vating polish. **Rubber** boots should just be rinsed under a cold tap.

**Trainers and gym shoes** Make sure gym or training shoes are completely dry before cleaning. Sponge off any dirt before whitening with a proprietary product. Most trainer manufacturers do not recommend machine-washing trainers, as it can weaken the support structures in the sole of the shoe. If you do wash trainers, ensure that any mud or dirt has been scraped off first.

Aerosol products are available to deal with smelly trainers.

**Walking boots and shoes**

Treat with regular applications of leather food to keep them waterproof, and occasional applications of dubbin, which will keep them flexible as well as adding further waterproof protection.

**Work boots**

Work boots should be cleaned immediately after wear as neglect will cause the leather to crack and the stitches to break. Remove mud, brush well and apply polish. From time to time, apply dubbin to keep the boots flexible. If you can afford two pairs and wear each of them only every other day they will last more than twice as long as shoes you wear day in, day out.

**Bags**

*Fabric* These can be washed, either by hand or in a machine. Use a grease solvent to remove marks, then wipe over with a damp cloth and allow to dry away from direct heat. If the fabric is really dirty, and not too delicate, use a nail-brush and soapflake solution. Scrape or wipe off the soapy residue, then wipe over with a cloth and leave to dry naturally. It is a good idea to spray a new fabric bag with a protector before using it, to help repel dirt.

*Reptile skin* This needs dusting very carefully in order not to loosen scales. An occasional application of hide food applied sparingly and rubbed in carefully will help to maintain its sheen.

*Leather* When removing from storage, and after use, brush well to remove dust and apply a thin coat of hide food. To clean, use a damp cloth rubbed over a glycerine soap tablet, then wipe with a warm damp cloth.

---

Leather handbags will stay cleaner if given a coating of shoe polish, which must be very well rubbed in to prevent it coming off on clothes.

---

*Straw/cane* Use neat washing-up liquid on dirty or sticky marks, then wipe over with a damp cloth wrung out of cold water and leave to dry. Do not use warm water, which could cause the straw to distort. If the straw/cane is reasonably firm, you could apply an aerosol cleaner to help protect against dirt, but make sure it is thoroughly dry before using the bag.

**Luggage** Hard luggage should be sponged over with a solution of washing-up liquid, rinsed and dried. A spray of cleaner/polish will help to protect the surface. Soft luggage may need an upholstery shampoo or a spray powder cleaner that brushes off.

Scratches on hard luggage are almost impossible to remove. Damage to soft luggage usually needs a professional repair; take it to a luggage shop for a price estimate.

When storing luggage put a couple of sugar lumps in it. These will absorb musty smells until you need the cases again.

# Chapter 6
# Outdoor cleaning

House exteriors

Gardens

Cars

Bicycles

Camping and caravanning

Keeping the exterior of your house clean is important, not only to maintain appearance but also to keep your property in good condition and functioning properly. The garden and all the things you use in it, such as tools, garden furniture and window boxes, need regular attention too. Cleaning cars and bicycles regularly allows you to keep an eye out for rust developing and small repairs that need doing.

## House exteriors

Make a positive resolution each spring to walk round the outside of your house and garden and note what needs doing. Use binoculars to check the roof and chimneypots – from the other side of the street or a neighbour's garden if necessary. Care of the exterior of flats is usually the responsibility of the landlord, an agent or an association of those who live in the block. Make sure that the exterior is checked annually.

*Exterior walls*    On the whole these do not need cleaning unless you live near the sea and find that salt has an adverse effect on a painted finish. You could wash exterior walls yourself but this is a laborious and tiring task and it is probably better to call in a professional firm with appropriate equipment or, in the case of painted walls, to have them repainted at regular intervals.

*Exterior windows and conservatories*    While you or your window-cleaner probably clean the glass on a regular basis (see 'Windows', page 120), the frames also need attention. Wash them over with a solution of household cleaner, paying particular attention to the underside of sills, where dirt can build up.

Check for gaps. Where the underside of the sill joins the wall is an area that is not instantly visible. Use a sealant to fill gaps and check wooden sills for rotting or splitting, which may mean replacing or repairing.

Check putty round the glass. Damaged areas should be chipped out and replaced before the putty falls out. Unless you have a good head for heights, upstairs windows are probably best repaired by a builder or glazier.

See also 'Greenhouses', page 172.

## Airbricks

Airbricks prevent damp from entering the home at floor level and also offer under-floor ventilation. They should be kept clear and free of débris. If they are silted up, wash them with a detergent solution, using a small wire brush to clear the holes – a teapot spout brush is about the right size.

At the same time check that the damp-proof course has not been bridged by a build-up of soil. If it has, remove the soil so that the course is completely clear.

## Drains

These should be inspected regularly; certainly more than once a year. Ground-level drain gullies should be cleared when débris builds up. Lift off the grid and use a trowel to scoop out what has collected.

Drains should only need to be cleaned twice a year, and if they are very clogged up and dirty it could make sense to call in a professional drain-cleaning firm. To clean them yourself, you may wish to use household bleach – this will remove grease, kill germs and get rid of smells. However, there are environmental arguments against the use of bleach (see Appendix I, Chemicals in cleaning products). An alternative mixture for pouring down drains is a solution of caustic soda (a handful to a bucket of hot water). It is important to wear gloves. If the drain is blocked, repeat the pouring until it looks clear. Note that many drain blockages are caused by unsuitable waste being put down the kitchen sink (see 'Blocked sinks', page 53).

Check manhole covers to see that they can be lifted easily. If they are cracked, replace them with new ones to prevent soil getting in. Use the caustic soda solution to clean the underside of the manhole cover, but avoid getting it on grass, flower beds or surrounding patio. You may need two people to hold the cover over the drain to ensure this.

The roots of nearby trees can sometimes grow into an outside drain and cause blocking. (For this reason, never plant new trees near drains.) If you suspect this to be the cause of a problem, call in a professional firm to deal with it – and if the tree belongs to a neighbour, give them the bill.

***Downpipes and gutters***

Gutters collect débris easily. Silt and soil form a breeding ground for weeds and grass,which can block the gutters, causing water to run down the walls and generate dampness on the outside and inside of the house.

To check gutters, use a ladder – but do not lean it against the gutter, which will not be strong enough to support it. Fit a ladder-stay, which will hold it slightly away from the wall.

Plug the downpipe with rags to prevent any débris you flush from the gutter getting into it and causing a blockage. If you are repainting the gutter protect the ground below from splashes using old sheets or plastic sheeting. (Do not stand the ladder on plastic sheeting or it may slip.)

Use a trowel to clear the débris from the gutter and save it for compost; the bird lime that will inevitably have accumulated makes it a good growing medium.

**Plastic** gutters can then be washed out using a solution of detergent. There is no need to rinse. If you find, after you have sloshed your bucket of cleaning liquid through it, that water collects at any point in the gutter, it means that the gutter is sagging and brackets need to be either tightened or replaced.

For **metal** gutters (now becoming rare), use a wire brush to scrape off any rust. Wash out and when dry touch up any bare metal with a rust inhibitor and apply a coat of zinc chromate primer, followed by a coat of bituminous paint.

---

**Ladder lore**

Before using any ladder check its condition, especially if it is made of wood and has been stored outdoors. If rungs are loose or wood has split, get rid of it and either buy or hire a new one. You need a good ladder to carry out exterior checks and it is a false economy to use one that is not safe. When buying a new ladder consider whether a platform or tower would be more use (for example, for major exterior work such as repointing or repainting). A ladder with a stay that holds it away from the wall is useful, as is an attachment for holding a bucket or tools. Ladders also come with adjustable legs for use on uneven ground and with suction feet to prevent it from moving on smooth ground.

Take care when setting up a ladder. You need a good firm base, so if you are working from soft earth get a solid board for the legs to rest on. The distance from the foot of the ladder to the base of the wall should be about a quarter of the height of the ladder.

As a general rule, avoid doing ladder work in windy weather. In any case, tie the ladder to a firm support at the sides and base so that it will not slide sideways. This is particularly important with lightweight aluminium ladders.

---

If your gutters regularly become clogged up it could be worth fitting them with a wire gutter covering, which prevents large pieces of débris from getting in. You will still have to check regularly for soil and weed growth.

Check that downpipes are not blocked at the top or at any point down the length by tipping a bucket of water down. If there is a blockage, dislodge it with either a length of strong wire, a bamboo cane or any long, strong tool you can improvise. You can buy wire coverings to shield drainpipes from blockages.

To deter burglars, consider painting downpipes with sticky anti-climb paint, which will leave a distinctive mark if touched.

**Doormats** For doormats made of coir, sisal and other tough natural materials, nothing is better than a good beating, administered out of doors with a stiff brush. Stand clear of flying débris or wear a protective mask. Always allow mud to dry before brushing it off. Stains are difficult to get out of stiff-pile doormats but it is always worth a try, using warm water and washing-up liquid applied on an old robust washing-up brush. Some doormats are washable, but after washing usually need to be sprayed with an aerosol dirt-repellent. These carpet-like mats are found in many offices, and office cleaning suppliers should be able to sell you replacement aerosols (see 'Office equipment' in Addresses section).

## Gardens

Keeping a garden 'clean' may sound odd, but every garden includes non-growth areas and items that need to be kept free from dirt and from the inevitable encroachment of nature.

Outdoor dustbins need not be cleaned as frequently as indoor bins. An outdoor tap and hose are probably the best tools for cleaning a dustbin. Leave the bin to dry completely before you put in a new bin liner. Dustbins stay cleaner (and refuse collectors prefer it) if you always use a dustbin liner for rubbish.

**Dustbins**

Wipe along the clothes lines with a damp cloth before each use. Dried-on bird droppings may need treating with washing-up liquid. Lubricate the moving parts of a rotary dryer with light machine oil every few months. If rust develops, rub down to bare metal with wire wool and apply a suitable outdoor paint.

**Clothes lines and rotary dryers**

The main problem with garden paths is weed growth, which is unsightly and can cause whatever the path is made from to break up. If you are not able to remove the weeds manually, use either a spot weedkiller (electric ones, which work by giving the plant a shock, are now available) to deal with individual weeds, or apply a path weedkiller, which should kill existing weeds and prevent re-growth for anything from several months to a year. Follow the instructions regarding small children and pets carefully. Wash out the container you use to apply the weedkiller several times immediately after use.

**Paths, steps and patios**

Dirt and grime on paving and concrete can be removed with either a proprietary cleaner or a solution of household bleach (120ml to 5 litres cold water). This is just as effective as, and a lot cheaper than, proprietary patio cleaners. Try to find a source of large sizes of whatever you use to clean the patio – this will save a lot of money. A cash-and-carry should sell industrial containers; otherwise contact a local institution (e.g. a school or community hall) to see whether they can get you supplies. Use a stiff-bristled broom or a scrubbing brush to brush it over the surface, leave for a few minutes and rinse with clean water. Another option for cleaning patios is to hire a high-pressure water-sprayer. Wear goggles during use and make sure the liquid doesn't get on lawns or flower beds.

Where there is a build-up of algae (highly dangerous as it is slippery) use a liquid house-hold cleaner containing bleach and make sure that every speck is removed. Do not use neat bleach to kill algae. For mildew, see page 37.

If after cleaning you find cracks in the patio or paving, use an exterior filler applied on a trowel to repair them.

**Drives** Clean concrete or paving stones in the same way as paths, steps and patios. Where there are oil stains use a proprietary paintbrush cleaner followed by rinsing with a hose and clear water. However, such treatment will not remove soaked-in oil on porous concrete: replacement, perhaps with an area of gravel which can itself be replaced as necessary, is the only real solution. Nor is the treatment suitable on asphalt, where sugar soap mixed according to the packet instructions should be used to shift stains.

**Gates and fences** Repair or replace any sections that have become damaged. For wood, use a stiff brush to clear attached débris, then apply an exterior wood preservative. For wrought iron, rub down any rust patches with steel wool and touch up with a rust inhibitor. If necessary, repaint with a suit-able weatherproof product.

**Greenhouses** If greenhouse glass is not clean, it will prevent the maximum amount of light getting in and plants will suffer. A clear-out once a year in the autumn will also prevent pests and diseases building up. Remove all plant débris, dead matter, leaves and rubbish first.

Scrub down the glass and frame, inside and out, plus any staging, using a solution of greenhouse disinfectant. Use a plastic plant label to remove dirt lodged in crevices around the edges of the glass.

When cleaning the roof glass you may find it easier to use a soft broom. Clean and sterilise pots and put old compost to use elsewhere in the garden.

An alternative way to rid the greenhouse of pests is to fumigate it. To do this check the cubic capacity (measure height × width × length) and purchase the appropriate quantity of fumigation pellets or a canister. Use masking tape to block any gaps in the greenhouse, then follow the instructions for fumigation.

***Sheds***

Choose a fine day to clear out your shed. Use the opportunity to get rid of things you do not use and products that have lost their labels or are past their use-by date.

When it is empty, use a long-handled brush to dust the roof and walls, giving any spiders the chance to run for their lives, and then sweep the floor.

If your shed is in an extremely dank part of the garden, or the wood is in permanent contact with moist soil, you may need to rub down the outside of the shed with fine steel wool and apply a coat of preservative annually.

Check the roofing felt and secure any area that has come loose. Replace the felt if it becomes damaged.

***Garden furniture***

Whether you keep it indoors or out, garden furniture needs care according to the material it is made from.

You will keep garden furniture cleaner if your protect it from adverse weather. You can buy plastic covers to fit all shapes from canopied swing seats to simple benches; but even if you use covers always store cushions and upholstery indoors or in a shed.

*Tubular metal* After the winter, carefully open folding chairs and loungers. If the hinges are stiff, use an aerosol lubricant; otherwise apply a drop of light oil, taking care not to get it on any fabric.

Wipe over the frame with a damp cloth wrung out of washing-up liquid solution, then apply a little wax polish to give a shine.

Covers are usually rot-proof canvas or plastic and just need wiping over with a damp cloth. Mend any tears with a patch or strong thread, and replace any covers that are too worn to be safe.

*Cast iron and steel* Oil hinges and treat any rust patches or chips with a proprietary rust remover. Then paint with a metal primer followed by exterior-quality gloss paint.

An enamelled finish just needs wiping over or hosing down with clear water.

*Wood* Remove dust with a soft cloth, then use fine steel wool or glasspaper to smooth the surface. Dust again, then apply a lacquer seal or exterior-quality varnish, which will last for years unless the furniture legs are in contact with moist soil throughout the winter.

*Hardwood* will withstand all weathers but will change colour unless sealed. If it is sealed (whether DIY or bought) you will need to rub it down each autumn and apply a fresh coat of seal to see it through the winter.

If you prefer the natural colour change that occurs without seal, you will need to remove any marks which appear, using steel wool rubbed in the direction of the grain. If the colour is not to your liking you can lighten it with a proprietary wood bleach.

---

Never use creosote on garden chairs as it will come off on clothes.

Wood furniture that is left outside during winter should be stood on wood blocks so that the feet are not in constant contact with damp ground.

---

*Cane* must be brought indoors during winter, otherwise the bindings may rot from exposure to constant wet weather. A shed or garage is a suitable place to store it as a heat source will cause it to split. Rub down and paint with clear polyurethane varnish to maintain appearance. (See also page 115.)

*Plastic* Clean with a solution of detergent or washing-up liquid, using an old toothbrush to get dirt out of cracks. Rinse well, using a hose if possible. Dry with old towels to prevent streaking and apply an aerosol polish to give some protection.

## Garden ornaments

Garden ornaments made from lead or stone need no cleaning.

Marble should be cleaned with a solution of household soap and water plus 60ml ammonia to the bucketful. Swab with a clean, soft cloth but note that this will remove any polish, so if you want a shine the marble will need to be repolished.

## Garden tools

After use, either push tools through a pile of sand to remove the dirt, or scrape off as much mud as possible (it may be easier if you leave it to dry first). Store with cutting edges and

175

prongs off the ground, and at the end of the gardening season clean all tools thoroughly and apply a coating of machine oil to keep them in good condition through the winter.

**Lawnmowers** If electric, remove from the electricity supply before cleaning. Use a piece of stick or bamboo cane to scrape off grass and dirt, clean out the air filter and clean and sharpen the blades. Oil non-electric mowers according to the manufacturer's instructions.

**Tubs and window boxes** Terracotta and porous stone should be hosed with clear water; plastic and painted finishes can be scrubbed with a solution of household detergent. Rinse interiors thoroughly before replacing, or renewing, compost.

**Ponds** Ponds should only be cleaned out if there is evidence of disease in fish or plants or if there is so much vegetation that the pond is choked with débris. Draining the pond is usually sufficient – drastic cleaning could harm plants and fish.

First decide what you are going to do with any fish or plants while cleaning is in progress. They should be kept in their existing water, perhaps in a child's paddling pool or other safe container. Cover with netting to keep out pets.

Drain the pond completely. Some old concrete ponds have plugs; otherwise you will have to siphon out the water to lower ground with a hose or pump, or bale it out. Scoop out any débris and remove any encrusted dirt. If the pond has a liner, take great care not to puncture it with sharp tools or your shoes.

When the pond is clean, fill it up with rain or tap water; leave overnight for the chlorine in the tap water to evaporate. Trim back any plants which have got too big and replant them in aquatic plant pots containing clay soil or special compost. Return the fish to the pond in plastic bags of the water in which they have been resting. Leave the bags suspended in the new water for an hour or so until both water temperatures are the same; then release them.

## Swimming pools

Filtering removes dirt, and chemicals are used to oxidise bacteria. Your pool supplier or installer will be able to advise you on the appropriate products suitable for the filtration system of your pool. Skimming fallen leaves off the surface with a small fishing net on a long stick will stop these being sucked into the traps and clogging up the filtration system.

Machines are available to 'vacuum' the base and sides of the pool automatically, certainly less back-breaking than attempting to do the job manually. Details should be supplied at the time of installation.

## Barbecues

Before cooking, scrape off any old food with a wire brush. You may find it easier to burn off the residue before scraping, by lighting the barbecue for a short time. Make sure you allow it to cool sufficiently.

## Tombstones

These can become covered with moss and lichen, so that any inscription or design is illegible. Take care with cleaning: tombstones are made from a number of different types of stone, some of which are very porous and easy to damage. Use a bucket of soapy water and a soft-bristled brush to scrub gently.

If the growth is so bad that a chemical solution is needed, take advice from a monumental mason, as chemicals react in different ways on different types of stone.

If you live a long way from a tombstone you would like tended, a local funeral director will often undertake the task for a fee.

## Cars

Keeping your car clean helps maintain its value as well as ensuring it looks good.

***Exteriors*** Car bodywork can be cleaned either in an automatic car wash or by hand. Make sure before you start that all doors and windows and the sunroof are tightly closed.

A car wash will shampoo the bodywork and apply a coating of wax, but will not get into any crannies or dirt traps and will not polish chrome.

You can do a better job by hand, though it will take time and effort. Use a hose or buckets of water to remove mud and grit.

Next, use a grit-free cloth and a bucket of detergent solution to wash over the whole of the car's bodywork, starting with the roof and working down. Alternatively you can use a proprietary car-washing kit consisting of a soft brush on the end of a hose, which siphons water up from a bucket into the brush head.

Strictly speaking, detergent should not be used on the bodywork of vehicles, as the paintwork is porous unless polished with wax, and detergent will strip the protective coating. However, plain water does not shift grease. For this reason manufacturers have had to improve their rust-proofing techniques, and car paints are quite tough these days. The detergent used should be a weak solution of something like washing-up liquid or a product from a car accessory shop.

Remove traces of tar with neat white spirit applied on a soft cloth.

Polishing is not essential but helps to protect the metal. Some polishes can be dissolved in a bucket of water and poured over the metal; they may dry shiny or need to be buffed with a chamois leather. Others are applied by hand.

**Chrome** just needs washing over and rubbing with a dry cloth. If you choose to apply a chrome polish make sure that it is well rubbed in, otherwise it will come off on people's hands.

Any **rust spots** should be treated with a rust inhibitor, then touched up with the correct colour car paint.

**Windows and windscreens** should be cleaned with a chamois leather wrung out of a bucket of soapy water. Rinse and polish well to avoid streaking. (A 'wiper' blade is useful.) You can buy a special brand of glass protector, Clearshield, which puts a dirt-resisting layer over the glass and keeps it cleaner for longer, particularly in muddy or dusty conditions (see Chapter 9, Products that work).

*Interiors*

Remove all rubbish from the car floor and the ashtrays, then use the attachments on your vacuum cleaner to get into nooks and crannies where dust and dirt accumulate. If you do not have a garage with a power point you will need either an extension lead or a small, battery-run vacuum cleaner. Use a spray cleaner and polish on the dashboard, glove compartment and any other hard surfaces.

If the upholstery is leather, wipe it with a damp cloth which has been rubbed over a tablet of glycerine soap. Do not rinse as the glycerine helps keep leather soft. Occasionally apply a little hide food to maintain suppleness but make sure it is rubbed in well and will not come off on people's clothes.

## Bicycles

These need cleaning little and often so that dirt does not build up on the frame or moving parts. Lubricate moving parts with a light, Teflon-based oil (ask at your local bicycle repair shop), once or twice a week. These oils do not attract dirt in the way a heavy oil does.

Clean the chain and sprockets with paraffin applied on a toothbrush (for the chain) and a 3-inch (7.5-cm) paintbrush (which should fit neatly between the sprockets). Clean the gear mechanism using paraffin on a 1-inch (7.5-cm) paintbrush. To clean the frame use a solution of washing-up liquid; work up a good lather, then rinse off. Do not use a hosepipe as the powerful jet of water could wash out the bearings, which are close to the surface. Dry with a soft cloth and just before everything is dry, spray the moving parts with light oil. Keep oil away from the brake pads and the rims of the wheels.

Protect leather saddles from the wet by tying plastic bags over them. Give the saddle an occasional coating of saddle soap to keep it soft and protect it. Vinyl saddles just need wiping with a damp cloth.

## Camping and caravanning

Camping and caravanning require extra effort on the cleaning front. Caravans – even the larger luxury variety – provide limited space compared to even the smallest apartment, so you need to clean and wash up pretty frequently. Keep contents to a minimum and use a hand-held vacuum cleaner or a dustpan and brush after meals to remove any crumbs which could attract mice or bugs.

A similar approach is applicable to camping, although on the whole basic housework is not on the agenda. It is important to wash up immediately after each meal, since facilities on some sites are fairly basic and the longer you leave food to congeal the more diffi-cult – and tedious – it will be to remove, particularly if there is no hot water. Bear in mind that you will possibly be sharing washing-up facilities with several hundred other people.

Keep food in sealed containers or off the ground and out of the reach of insects and animals.

*Gore-Tex*  This a breathable, waterproof fabric used to make outdoor clothing, rucksacks and tents. It should be treated with care and washed only with the specialist product G-clean (supplier details in garment), following the instructions supplied with the item. Gore-Tex should be ironed to keep the pores closed and waterproof. You can also have it reproofed (see 'Outdoor clothing' in Addresses section).

**Rucksacks**

Like tents, these are made from different fabrics and will come with care instructions. Again, they should be dried out when possible. Unpack yours completely as often as you can and shake out the dust which will accumulate in the bottom and the pockets. After a particularly gruelling trip, have it cleaned professionally. A specialist camping shop will advise who can do this.

**Tents**

Tents are made from a variety of fabrics and will come with care instructions on purchase. The most important thing to remember is that a tent must be *dry* when stored, even for a short time – a damp tent may develop mildew, which may be impossible to eradicate. (See 'Mildew', page 37.) If you have to leave a camping pitch with a wet tent, make sure you erect it again as soon as possible, even if it is raining. If, at the end of a camping holiday, you have to go home with a wet tent, put it up in your garden or, if there is no alternative, your living room until it is absolutely dry before putting it away.

# Pets and pests

## Animals and hygiene

There is probably some truth in saying if you want to keep your home spotless, do not keep pets. While they can bring lots of pleasure to their owners, they also shed hairs, sleep on furniture and never wipe their feet!

Uninvited creatures can do more serious damage. Mice, rats and invasions of insects can all wreak havoc in your home. It is sometimes necessary to call in pest control professionals to get rid of them.

## Cats and dogs

The main problem is the hairs they shed. You can buy special gadgets for removing pet hairs from upholstery and carpets where a vacuum cleaner has not succeeded, but an equally successful solution is to wrap sticky tape (Sellotape or masking tape) round your fingers – sticky-side out – and attack affected areas. Replace the tape as it becomes clogged up with hairs.

Regular grooming of animals will remove loose hairs and entangled débris. The earlier in their lives you start grooming them, the less they will resent it.

Bath dogs when necessary; those fond of rolling in smelly matter will require frequent bathing. It is possible to bath cats if you get them used to it from an early age, but on the whole they are good at grooming themselves.

Try to train cats and dogs to sleep in one place, on bedding which can be washed. There is no need to buy anything special – old jumpers, worn blankets or picnic rugs make perfectly good bedding. Just remember to wash it regularly.

Cats and dogs are easily house-trained as long as you do it when they are young. If accidents do occur, treat the stain accordingly (see pages 46 and 47).

Walk your dog regularly and make sure he or she performs somewhere suitable (some councils provide special areas for dogs' excreta) or take a poop scoop and plastic bag with you so you can clear up any mess.

For cats the best solution if possible is to fit a cat flap so that they can attend to matters outdoors. If not, or in the event of your cat being ill, provide a litter tray. You will get less smell around the house if you use the sort that has a 'lid' and looks rather like a small dog kennel. The litter tray must be cleaned out daily. Use hot water and a little disinfectant, then rinse thoroughly. Provide fresh litter every day.

If your house smells strongly and unacceptably of cat or dog ask your vet to recommend a deodorising product, but be careful where you spray it – some may affect carpets or upholstery. As always, test on a small inconspicuous area first.

Fleas can also become a household problem. To clear your home of them use flea spray or powder. Flea products are available from pet shops and some chemists but you will get a stronger, more effective (and more expensive) brand from your vet, which is likely to work better. First spray (or dust) some of it inside your vacuum cleaner bag so that any live fleas or pupae collected by it are killed. Then vacuum thoroughly all around the house, using tools such as the crevice attachment to get into nooks and crannies. Also vacuum any furniture on which the cat has slept, including beds.

Treat the cat or dog with flea spray at the same time as cleaning the house. Most flea sprays are toxic, so apply it out of doors, following the manufacturer's instructions.

Once the animal is clear of fleas you can try to get it to wear a flea collar, but unfortunately cats and dogs can pick up fleas anywhere at any time and you should be prepared to deal with the problem on a regular basis.

A pill has been developed, for cats and dogs, to prevent flea infestation. It causes the animal to develop a substance in the bloodstream which prevents fleas reproducing themselves. Ask your vet for advice on whether your pet needs it.

Injections against fleas are also possible, although at present they are only available for cats. This may not solve the problem totally but will certainly help.

If the flea infestation is too bad for you to treat yourself call in a pest control contractor (see 'Pest control' in Addresses section).

## Small pets

Gerbils, hamsters and mice need to be kept scrupulously clean if their cages are kept indoors or they will smell, and the animals will be disturbed by their unhygienic environment.

Dirty cages could also be a source of disease, as bacteria may be transmitted by flies in hot weather, for example.

Change the bedding regularly, together with whatever you use for the floor of the cage. You should clean the toilet area daily and the material in the sleeping area once or twice a week. The smaller the cage the more quickly it will get dirty.

Smell is less of a problem for animals such as guinea pigs and rabbits, whose hutches are generally outdoors. However, they, too, should be kept in hygienic and comfortable conditions.

Once a month clean all hutches and cages thoroughly. Take out everything and wash and dry the area. Make sure you have somewhere safe to put the pet while this is going on – especially if you also have a cat.

## Caged birds

Daily cleaning is needed to remove droppings, seed husks, any uneaten matter and moulted feathers. The easiest way to get rid of them is to line the base of the cage with old newspaper and a layer of sand which collects the droppings and can just be slid into a disposal bag.

Once a week clean the cage thoroughly. If your birds have an exercise period each day, do the cleaning while they are flying. Otherwise find somewhere safe for them – a cat's wicker travelling basket is useful.

Remove all the bits and pieces in the cage and wash and dry it. Check any toys, mirrors and so on for cracks or sharp edges and remove anything that is damaged.

Wipe over the inside of the cage with damp kitchen paper, including the perches. Check whether the perches have become too smooth and, if so, use sandpaper to give a rough surface for the bird's feet.

If you have an aviary the cleaning procedure is the same but will be more onerous because of the larger number of birds involved. Use a stiff broom to wash down concrete floors. If the floor is bare earth, rake off as much of the droppings as you can.

## Fish

Cold-water fish should be cleaned out when their tank starts to look silted up. Some types are dirtier than others and need more frequent cleaning. Put out bowls of water some hours before you clean the tank so that it reaches room temperature and some of the chlorine can evaporate. Just before cleaning, catch the fish (you can buy a small soft net at aquatic retailers) and put them into one of the bowls, making sure that it is sufficiently deep for them not to leap out.

Remove the pebbles or gravel from the base of the tank and wash under running water until all slime and algae have gone. A metal colander makes a good container for this as it stops small pieces of gravel slipping down the plughole and blocking the waste outlet.

Scrub off the deposit that has formed on the sides of the tank using warm water and a soft brush. Rinse any live weed and replace it if it looks past its best.

Return the gravel to the tank, reposition weed and ornaments, fill up and return the fish to it. With open-topped tanks, keeping the water level up will keep the fish cleaner.

Tropical fish require the same cleaning procedure but it is essential that the fish are kept in heated water while out of the tank. Cleaning out tropical fish tanks is a job best done by two people – one to do the dirty work and the other to keep boiling kettles of water (a bit like home midwifery) and checking the temperature of the water in which the fish are stored. With even a smallish tank the cleaning procedure can take some time.

When cleaning out the fish tank watch out for your cat, which may be able to get at the fish in their bowl.

---

Pets, especially neighbours' dogs and cats, can do damage to gardens. You can apply an aerosol pet deterrent to fences, doorways, gateposts, window boxes, dustbins and plant stems. Aerosols should remain effective for a few days in dry weather.

Electric pet deterrents, which administer a slight but harmless electric shock, are one alternative. You can also get cat repellent spray containing natural aromatic oils, or a barrier deterrent consisting of a web of soft plastic spikes, from organic gardening suppliers.

## Household pests

No one wants pests in their home, but they have a way of creeping in undetected. Some you can deal with yourself (see Chapter 9, Products that work); for others you may require professional help. Nip the problem in the bud as soon as you discover it, or you could end up with an unpleasant infestation.

*Mice*  Mice enjoy the warmth and shelter of buildings and are not fazed by human company. They can cause damage to the structure of a home because of their need to nibble, which can destroy electric cables, gas and water pipes. They will contaminate food and they carry a number of diseases, including food poisoning.

Mouse traps are suitable only if you do not have a large colony in the house. Otherwise it is best to call in the pest control unit. Mice have become immune to many of the over-the-counter poisons you can buy and those provided by pest control agencies are stronger. Once the mice have been disposed of, block up holes with wire wool and quick-setting cement.

*Pigeons*  Pigeons are very dirty birds and can transmit diseases to humans. If they have found a way into your loft, the local authorities are able to deal with them, so contact your local environmental health department.

*Rats*  Rats, oddly enough, are easier to get rid of than mice and less keen on domestic environments, preferring sewers and rubbish dumps. Like mice, they chew things and will damage the structure of a home and also spread disease and food poisoning. To get rid of them either buy rat poison or call in pest control experts.

Do not allow the problem to escalate once you have discovered mice or rats.

Squirrels like the warmth and comfort of **_Squirrels_**
domestic lofts and cause both damage and noise
once they move in. They love to eat the casing
on electrical cable, and will make nests out of
loft insulation material. You cannot kill them
yourself since they require a strong pesticide
which can only be used by people trained under
the Control of Pesticides Regulations (1986).

Once you have called in the experts and they
have returned to pick up any dead animals, make
sure no bodies are left which could decay and
smell, then block up the eaves, using chicken
wire so that air can still circulate in the area.

## Insects

For those insect problems that do not demand professional attention,
the requisite insecticidal products (see Chapter 9, Products that
work) are available from chemists, hardware shops, pet shops or vets.

You need first to find the ants' nest: watch **_Ants_**
where they move when they are carrying food.
Pour a kettle of boiling water over the nest, then
puff an insecticidal powder into the hole. Paint
insecticidal lacquer around their most frequently used door thresholds and where the
floor meets the wall.

While not classified as pests, bees can cause **_Bees_**
problems if they don't belong to you but decide
to swarm in your garden. They are a protected
species so to get rid of them you will need to
either contact your local council (which will
probably refer you to the local beekeepers' association), or get in touch with a registered bee
'contractor' (see 'Pest control' in Addresses section), who may be obliged to gas the swarm if
there is no alternative.

**Carpet beetles**   Carpet beetles damage carpets and bedding by biting the threads in them. You need an appropriate insecticide to kill the larvae and beetles, and damaged items should also be sprayed with a carpet beetle control product.

To prevent their return, check you have no old birds' nests or dead birds in the loft or under the eaves. Vacuum the shelves and floors in your airing cupboard, and lift carpets and underlay to vacuum the floor below.

**Clothes moths**   These not only ruin clothes but can damage carpets and upholstery. Be careful how you store woollens and fur coats, which are favourite breeding grounds. If you are storing them away, put a sachet of moth-repellent in with them.

Keep your loft free of unused fabric or carpet, and at the first sign of moths, spray upholstery, carpets and clothes with mothproofer.

**Cockroaches**   Cockroaches carry various diseases including food poisoning. They are nocturnal and will eat almost anything. Use an aerosol insecticide to kill them, but if this fails contact the environmental health department of your local authority.

**Dust mites**   These are virtually impossible to eradicate but you can keep them at bay by using a vacuum cleaner on mattresses when you change the sheets. Take care not to pull out any tufts or buttons.

The presence of dust mites does not mean your home is dirty. They are persistent pests. However, they can cause problems for people who are allergic to them and who may develop itching when in bed. You can buy anti-allergenic bedclothes, which may help. Consult your doctor, practice nurse or pharmacist about this.

**Fleas**   See page 185.

These transmit food poisoning and other diseases. Be scrupulously clean in the kitchen and do not leave refuse lying around. Keep the lids on bins, and clean them out frequently. Spray the inside with insecticide. Keep food covered or refrigerated at all times. If flies are a real problem, invest in an ultra-violet electric fly-killer of the type seen in some food shops. Remember that one teaspoon of waste left lying around will feed 200 houseflies!

*Flies*

Store pesticides out of reach of children and people with poor eyesight. Follow the instructions to the letter.

If you have a wasps' nest on your premises it is best to have it removed professionally, as DIY attempts with substances such as fillers can leave some of the holes unblocked. Your local council may offer a removal service (for a fee) or give you the name of a firm to contact (see also 'Pest control' in Addresses section). There are proprietary products you can spray on, but take care not to anger the wasps into stinging you while you are applying it.

*Wasps*

Wasps sting only when provoked, but provocation can be caused by children rushing around, for example. Don't attempt to swat wasps as this can also cause them to sting. Try to trap them with a jam jar or other container with a little diluted jam or beer in the base. Cover the container with paper held on with an elastic band and make a few holes in it with a pencil so the wasps can get in but will find it difficult to get out.

# Chapter 8

# Cleaning in special circumstances

Fire and flood damage

Infectious diseases and illness

Babies in the home

Cleaning for people with disabilities

## Fire and flood damage

It is vital to have insurance against fire or flood damage, so that if the worst does happen your home can be restored to its former habitable self as quickly as possible.

Before attempting to clean up after a fire or a flood, first ring your insurers to ask what action you can take without affecting your claim. They will need to send a loss adjuster to confirm the extent of damage and assess the amount they will have to pay out, but they may allow you to take remedial action before this, especially if you use the services of a professional firm which they recommend and which can report on the extent of the damage before starting work. Though it may be distressing, it does help if you photograph the damaged areas in some detail to provide a record before you start clearing up. Do not do anything which could jeopardise your claim and do not attempt to clean anything unless you are sure you can achieve a satisfactory result.

*Fire damage*    After a fire your home will not only look awful, with damage to flammable possessions and greasy black deposits on fixed surfaces, but also smell unpleasant, owing to fumes produced by the substances which have been burned. A professional cleaning firm should be able to supply you with a machine to deal with this.

In general, you are unlikely to be able to clear up yourself after a major fire, but if the damage is limited there are some things you can do. Tackle one room at a time and thoroughly wash the walls and ceiling. If flooring is not damaged too badly you can shampoo carpets and wash hard floors. It could be worth hiring a professional carpet cleaning machine, which will do a better job than a small domestic one. You will also need to wash all items which show signs of damage. Washable fabrics should be laundered on a heavy-duty programme. You may prefer to use a launderette rather than put fire-damaged débris into your own machine.

If you have any advance warning of flooding in your area, move as many of your possessions off the ground floor as possible. Put sandbags along the bottoms of doors and over air bricks. Do not use electricity or gas or draw off any tap water until the authorities say it is safe to do so.

*Flood damage*

If your home is flooded, lift floor coverings so they will dry more quickly and leave doors, windows and built-in cupboards open.

You will need to employ a professional cleaning firm to extract water from carpets and upholstery, and they will provide heated blowing machines to dry them out after this. An anti-bacterial product is usually used to wash down walls and hard surfaces, and this will also help reduce smell. The firm may ask you to turn up the central heating to aid the drying process.

Remember that drying-out can take months, so do not redecorate immediately. To avoid dry rot, allow at least six months before re-laying floor coverings.

---

**Frozen and burst pipes**

- If a pipe has frozen, turn off the stopcock. Thaw the pipe, using a hair-dryer, hot water bottle or towel soaked in very hot water, along the pipe's length from the tap end towards the tank. Turn off the boiler and call in a plumber.
- For a burst pipe, again turn off the stopcock. If the burst is on a pipe leading from a storage tank, try to prevent all the water escaping. If you cannot stop the flow, turn on all the cold taps in the house. Turn off the central heating and any immersion heaters and call a plumber.
- Turn your stopcock once a year to make sure it still moves. If it does not, call in a plumber to loosen it.

---

***Roof damage*** If a storm or heavy snowfall damages your roof, use sheets of hardboard, plastic or corrugated iron to keep out rain and snow. Shovel any snow off the loft floor before it melts and drips through the ceilings below. Check gutters for blockages.

To reduce the risk of damage, check roofs, chimneys and gutters for any weak spots before winter comes.

## Infectious diseases and illness

It is rare for a house to retain infection, even if someone living in it has been ill. However, if you are concerned that there may be a problem and someone vulnerable, like a pregnant mother, will be coming to your home, contact the environmental health department of your local authority and discuss the problem with staff there.

In cases of diseases like TB (which is highly infectious) or the presence of an invalid with suppurating wounds, contact the infection control nurse at your local hospital, who will be able to give advice on any related problems.

If someone in the household is incontinent and needs to wear pads or has dressings which need to be disposed of, consult the environmental health department of your local authority about arrangements for disposal. There is usually a special collection service for which you will be supplied with special disposal bags.

## Babies in the home

You do not need to be over-protective of babies. The adage that a peck of dirt taken in is healthier still holds good to some extent, although you should obviously take great care over sterilising bottles and washing hands and work surfaces before preparing food. There is no need to provide a clinical environment since in due course a baby has to get to grips with the real world. It is, however, important for both babies and young children that you do not leave any cleaning products in a place where they could find them and consume them. Never decant cleaning products into other containers which a child might recognise as a favourite food or drink.

For advice on laundering nappies, see page 146; for removing urine and vomit stains, see pages 46 and 47.

See also 'Plasticine and playdough', page 43; 'Toys', page 139; and Appendix II, Safety and first aid, page 213.

## Cleaning for people with disabilities

While cleaning may be more difficult and time-consuming for the physically disabled, it may still be possible using some of the aids available to make certain tasks easier.

The Disabled Living Foundation (see 'Cleaning for people with disabilities' in Addresses section) has displays in branches around Britain and a list of mail-order catalogues offering useful items. These include holders for brushes, cloths and scouring pads, washing-up brushes on suction cups, dishcloth wringers and window-cleaning gadgets. There are also extending handles for brooms and brushes, and telescopic wall mops. You can fit special trigger handles to aerosols to make them easier to use.

For laundry, using a wheeled trolley saves you having to bend and if your eyesight is poor you can get a Braille conversion for the knobs on your washing machine. There are even water-soluble bags for laundry which you can just put into the machine in one go.

You or any sick or disabled person in your household may be entitled to special services which give practical help with cleaning the home. The Chronically Sick and Disabled Persons Act 1970 entitles you to practical help with cleaning services if you are:

- substantially and permanently handicapped
- blind or partially sighted
- deaf or hard of hearings
- mentally ill
- mentally handicapped.

Your local branch of Age Concern (see 'Cleaning for people with disabilities' in Addresses section) will advise you on your entitlement and you may be eligible for a grant for equipment or help in making your home more cleaning-friendly.

Chapter 9
# Products that work

No list of cleaning products can claim to be comprehensive, but those shown here work well and are, on the whole, widely available. Most can be found in shops and supermarkets; for those that are mail-order only, see Addresses section for supplier details. Not listed are the own brands of supermarkets, DIY shops and department stores, which generally provide excellent value for money.

Bear in mind that it is vital to read instructions carefully and follow them to the letter – a product which appears suitable for a particular task could be inappropriate for the item you intend to clean. Follow the manufacturer's instructions for storing products – usually in a cool, dark, airy place – and throw them out if they start to look different from the way they did when bought, or don't seem to work properly. Whenever cleaning or using a new product for the first time, test it first on a small, inconspicuous patch and check for results.

If you own something like a Corian worktop or Amtico floor it is best to buy their recommended cleaning products, as using something else may cause damage which cannot be repaired.

Bear in mind that, on the whole, very cheap products are less good value than their more expensive counterparts. They are often diluted so you need to use more to get a good result.

| | |
|---|---|
| ***All-purpose cleaners (hard surfaces)*** | *Ajax Scourer • Astonish Cream Cleaner • Bar Keeper's Friend • Dettox Anti-bacterial Cleaner • Jeyes Kleen Off • Jif Mousse • Mr Muscle Kitchen Cleaner • Mr Muscle Professional Kitchen Cleaner • Mr Muscle Professional Multi-surface Cleaner • Mr Sheen • Pledge Soapy Wood Cleaner • White Wizard Spot Remover and All-Purpose Cleaner* |
| ***Bath and shower cleaners/ limescale removers*** | *Evo-Stik Grout Revive • Fernox Limescale Remover (taps) • Jeyes Kleen Off Bath Cleaner • Limelite Power Gel • Mr Muscle Bathroom Cleaner • Mr Muscle Professional Washroom Cleaner • Toilet Duck 100% Limescale Destroyer* |
| ***Car cleaners*** | *CarPlan All-season Screen Wash • CarPlan Kleen Up Upholstery Cleaner* |

| | |
|---|---|
| *Scotchgard* | **Carpet treatment to protect from dirt** |

*1001 Carpet Mousse • 1001 Carpet Shampoo • Bissell Aerosol Carpet Cleaner • Bissell Aerosol Upholstery Shampoo • Bissell Carpet Shampoo • Bissell Instant Cleaner (for pet and baby accidents – removes stains and deodorises) • Bissell Upholstery Shampoo • Glade Shake 'n' Vac • Kleeneze Carpet and Upholstery Shampoo • Vanish Carpet Shampoo • Vanish Mousse*

**Carpet and upholstery cleaners**

*Antiquax Chandelier Cleaner*

**Chandeliers**

*Brillo Soap Pads • Helping Hands Giant Dry-Cleaning Pad (for lampshades, blinds, wallpaper and fabrics suitable for dry-cleaning) • Microtex Professional Cleaning Cloth (no chemicals – use dry or damp to remove grease and other marks) • Minky All-Purpose Kitchen Cloth • Minky Clean 'n' Wipe Cloth • Minky Fast Wipes • Minky Floor and Wall Cloth • Minky Non-Stick Scouring Pads • Minky Scouring Pads • Minky Soak-Ups • Minky Window Cloth • Mr Muscle Spongy Scourers • Swiffer (long-handled cleaning mop that takes disposable electrostatic cloths) • Vileda Attractive (disposable electrostatic cloths, especially good for screens) • Vileda Dishcloth*

**Cloths and scourers**

*Astonish Cream Cleaner • Bar Keeper's Friend • Brillo Oven and Grill Pan Cleaner • Homecare 4 Hob • Homecare Hob Brite • Jeyes Kleen Off • Jeyes Kleen Off (microwaves and fridges) • Mr Muscle Oven Cleaner*

**Cooker cleaners**

*Oust Dishwasher and Washing Machine Cleaner*

**Dishwasher cleaner**

**Disinfectants**  *Dettol • Milton*

**Doorstep**  *Cardinal Self-shine Red Liquid (red doorsteps only)*
**cleaner**

**Drain cleaner**  *Manger's Caustic Soda*

**Floor cleaners**  *Johnson Klear (floor shine) • Marley Floor Cleaner*
**(including**  *• Marley Floor Gloss • Marley Floor Stripper •*
**strippers and**  *Ronuk Wax*
**waxes)**

**Furniture**  *Antiquax Furniture Cleaner (removes polish build-*
**cleaners/**  *up) • Mansion Aerosol Polish • Mansion Enriched*
**polishes**  *Cream • Mansion Wax Polish • Mr Sheen •*
*Renaissance Wax Furniture Polish (see 'Furniture*
*polish' in Addresses section) • Ronuk Wax •*
*Stephenson's Olde English Furniture Cream •*
*Stikatak Laminate Floor Cleaner*

**Glass cleaners**  *Clear-shield (puts a protective film on glass. See*
*'Glass' in Addresses section) • Mr Muscle Window*
*and Glass Cleaner • Windolene*

**Grate cleaner**  *Zebro Black Grate Polish*

**Hand and face**  *Glovelies • Marigold Bathroom Gloves • Marigold*
**protection**  *Kitchen Extra Life Gloves • Marigold Outdoor*
*Gloves • Sensitive Skin Washing-up Liquid •*
*Superglove Cotton Housework Gloves*

**Insect killers**  *Doff Wasp Nest Killer • Nippon Ant Killer • Raid*
*Ant and Cockroach Killer • Raid Ant Killer Powder*
*• Raid Fly and Wasp Killer • Raid Wasp Nest*
*Destroyer • Rentokil Crawling Insect and Ant Killer*
*• Rentokil Fly Papers • Rentokil Fly, Wasp and*
*Mosquito Killer • Rentokil Rodine C Rat and*
*Mouse Killer • Vapona Plug-in Flying Insect Killer*

*Goddard's Gold and Platinum Jewellery Cleaning
Liquid*

**Jewellery
cleaner**

*Vilene Iron Cleaner*

**Iron cleaner**

*These are too numerous to list in detail; the list that
follows is a small selection of the wide range available.
Laundry products divide roughly into pre-wash and
in-wash products, with specialist brands for hand
washing, net curtain whitening and so on. The range
of own brands is vast and quite often a supermarket
will disguise the fact that a product is an own brand
by giving it another name in addition to the
supermarket's name.*

**Laundry
products**

*When choosing a laundry product it is important to
read the instructions and make sure it is right for what
you are washing. For example, never use soapflakes in
a washing machine; the suds will cause a major
problem. Biological detergents, although excellent for
washing out stains, carry warnings that they should
not be used on items with zips and certain types of
finish. Use the amount recommended. More will not
improve the result while a cheeseparing less may not
get things clean.*

*For more advice on washing and products, see
under 'Laundry' in Addresses section.*

*Ariel Color • Ariel Handwash • Bounce (sheets for
tumble dryer) • Comfort Pure • Comfort Vitality
(softener) • Dreft (hand wash) • Dylon Super Wash
Booster • Dylon Colour Run • Fairy Snow (hand-
washing) • Glo White Go White Super Whitener •
Liquid Surf • Non-biological Fairy Automatic •
Surcare Automatic Washing Powder for Sensitive
Skins • Vanish In-wash Stain Remover • Woolite
(for woollens and delicates)*

*Domestos • Harpic • Jeyes Parazone • Toilet Duck
Liquid*

**Lavatory
cleaners**

**Lubricant (general purpose)**   *WD40*

**Marble cleaner**   *Antiquax Marble Wax*

**Metal cleaners**   *Brasso Liquid • Brasso Wadding • Goddard's Long Term Brass and Copper Polish • Maas Metal Polishing Cream*

**Mould cleaners**   *Cuprinol Fungal Spray • Cuprinol Mould Killer • Dettox Mould and Mildew Remover • Fungo (all-purpose, both indoors and outdoors. See 'Fungicidal treatment' in Addresses section) • Mystox (see 'Mildew' in Addresses section) • Polycell Mould Killer*

**Odour removers**   *(See also 'Pet products')*
*Febreze (removes smells from all fabrics and soft – not hard – surfaces) • Fresh Hands (a steel 'egg' for wiping hands; removes smell of foods such as fish and onion. See 'Hand deodoriser' in Addresses section) • Wonder Bar (removes food smells from hands)*

**Oven cleaner**   *Grillomat Oven and Grill Cleaner*

**Patio and drive cleaners**   *Mystox (see 'Mildew' in Addresses section)*

**Pet products**   *Bissell Instant Cleaner (to remove stains from and deodorise carpets and upholstery) • Bob Martin Flea and Tick Solution (for dogs) • Bob Martin Household Flea Spray • Bob Martin Silent Flea Spray for Cats • Simple Solution (removes pet stains and odours)*

**Scratch and mark removers**   *Colron Liquid Scratch Cover (wood repairs) • Colron Ring Remover • Topps Ring-Away • Topps Scratch Cover*

| | |
|---|---|
| Antiquax Silver Service • Goddard's Long Term Silver Pad • Goddard's Long Term Silver Polish • Goddard's Silver Dip • Silvo Tarnish Guard (wadding) | **Silver cleaners** |
| Mr Muscle Sink and Plughole Unblocker | **Sink cleaner** |

Shout Aerosol Stain Removing Spray • Shout **Stain removers**
Trigger Stain Removing Spray • Stain Devils (see
'Stain removers' in Addresses section):
    Number 2 (for blood, milk, ice-cream, egg,
    yoghurt and cream)
    Number 3 (for emulsion paint, nail varnish,
    correcting fluid, chewing gum, tar, all-purpose
    glues and furniture polish)
    Number 4 (for coffee, tea, cola, red wine, mould
    and writing ink)
    Number 5 (for grease, oils, shoe polish, ballpoint
    pen, felt-tip pen and unknown origin)
    Number 7 (for iron mould and rust)
    Number 10 (for grass, chocolate, cosmetics, gravy,
    curry and ketchup)
• Stikatak Carpet Stain Remover • Vanish Liquid
Stain Remover • Vanish Pre-wash Stain Remover •
Vanish Pre-wash Stain Stick

| | |
|---|---|
| Manger's De-Solv-It (see 'Stain removers' in Addresses section) | **Sticky label cleaner** |
| Absorb (cleaning spray) | **Textile cleaner** |
| Calgon | **Water softener** |

# Appendix I

# Chemicals in cleaning products

Consumer awareness of harmful chemicals, and concern about their effects, is increasing. In recent years many 'green' products have found their way on to shop shelves and, as with organic foods, have steadily risen in popularity. Most people know that chemicals are used in the production of food, but fewer realise that they are also found in household items that we take for granted – from carpets to computers, paints, perfumes and cleaning products. We are what we eat but we are also what we clean with.

It is estimated that our bodies contain hundreds of man-made chemicals – from pollution, food and the products we use. These may be damaging both the environment and our health: their effects are not yet fully understood and may have serious consequences for the future. There is evidence that people have developed allergies to certain household products because of the chemicals they contain. And today's homes with their draughtproofing, double glazing, fitted carpets and other contemporary comforts present a captive environment for pollutants and toxic substances.

In the case of food production, the use of pesticides is regulated and limits are set for harmful chemical contaminants. For other products, however, the legislation is inadequate. In recent years the UK and other European governments have made recommendations aimed at ending the discharge of hazardous chemicals into the environment, but these rely on voluntary action on the part of the industry rather than regulation, and in practice little has been done. For most chemicals in production, there is little or no safety information available. Nor is the industry required to inform consumers about what goes into their products. Most manufacturers are reluctant to disclose this information – perhaps partly because many of them produce cleaners as own brands and for other branded companies, and wish to keep product and customer details confidential.

## Health risks

The types of chemicals that are of particular concern are those known as 'persistent' (they do not biodegrade easily), 'bioaccumulative' (they build up in body tissues) and 'toxic'. Artificial musks, which are used as fragrances, are one type of persistent and bioaccumulative chemical frequently found in household cleaning products. Other common ingredients of these products are toxic. These include a group of chemicals called volatile organic compounds (VOCs), which give off fumes in the warmth of our homes and are found in a variety of petroleum-based substances, including synthetic furnishings, cleaning products, and building and decorating materials. VOCs can cause headaches, sinus congestion, nausea and fatigue.

The following are some of the problem chemicals found in everyday household cleaners.

- Solvents are associated with a variety of health problems, and can be inhaled or absorbed through the skin – which is why you should always wear household gloves when handling cleaning fluids.
- Ammonia, used for its disinfectant properties, is highly toxic, can exacerbate respiratory problems and is corrosive.
- Sodium hypochlorite, a constituent of most bleaches, can give off irritating fumes. Bleach should never be mixed with cleaning products that contain acids, as the chloramine gas formed by the resulting reaction is extremely harmful.
- Colouring and fragrances are added to virtually every cleaning product – one reason for the latter being to hide the smell of all the other chemicals. But many allergy problems, both from inhalation and contact with the skin, are associated with these fragrances.

Traditional cleaning substances, used until recent decades, were much simpler; the range available has proliferated hugely, reflecting a consumer preoccupation with 'super-cleanliness'. One product of this trend is anti-bacterial cleaners. There is now some concern that the sanitised environment these create can cause problems in itself: bacteria may develop a lack of resistance to the cleaning products, and our own immune systems could be depleted. There is growing support among scientists for the theory that this may account for the rise in the incidence of asthma and other allergies.

## Environmental effects

In response to today's consumer concern about harm to the environment, the same industry that gives us 'germ-busting' products is now offering a plethora of 'green' ones. The term is a loose one, however, and does not necessarily tell us what they contain. (For example, a product may be described as 'biodegradable'. In fact, virtually all ingredients biodegrade eventually; it is the *rate* of degradation that is important.)

Powerful chemicals are washed down our drains and into the sewage system, ending up in rivers, and the danger is that they do not break down fast enough to prevent them causing ecological harm. For example, surfactants (an ingredient of detergents, which unlike soap, are effective on grease in hard water) are not only toxic but can allow other harmful chemicals to penetrate living things. This means that it is important that they biodegrade quickly in order not to harm aquatic wildlife. Bleach is another very powerful chemical, which acts by sterilising organic matter. There is some concern, however, that its antibacterial action can inhibit the breakdown of sewage. Sodium hypochlorite can break down into compounds that are very toxic. Phosphates, also found in detergents and laundry products, cause 'eutrophication' – the overgrowth of algae, which chokes waterways and starves other waterlife of oxygen. 'EDTA', sometimes used as an alternative to phosphates, binds with toxic metals present in the environment, making them soluble and thereby returning them to the water system and the food chain.

In general, 'green' products are made from vegetable-based ingredients, which biodegrade more quickly than petroleum-based ones, and produce less pollution in the manufacturing process. Soaps break down quickly and safely, and are effective in soft-water areas. Some 'eco-friendly' ranges of cleaning products do not include bleach but offer cleaners that use acids to control bacteria. Such products generally use recyclable packaging.

## But do 'green' products work?

Obviously, this book is about cleaning – and as such is principally concerned with the effectiveness of the available cleaning products. Some products which claim to be environmentally friendly do not work as well as those containing potentially hazardous chemicals. How 'green' we want to be is a choice for each of us as an individual: this may mean a choice between adjusting our ideas of what we expect our cleaning products to do – and perhaps tolerating an acceptable, if less than perfect, result – or risking the possible harmful effects of a product that really does the job it claims to do.

## What you can do

If you are considering using environmentally friendly products, but standards of cleanliness are very important to you, it could be worth testing the brand you normally use against one claiming to be more ecologically friendly and seeing how effective the 'green' one is before making a choice. If you use concentrated products, look carefully at the amount you use: while these make good sense in terms of packaging, people tend to use more than the equivalent amount of the non-concentrated variety, thus increasing the volume of chemicals handled and released into the environment.

If you are genuinely concerned and want to 'go green', then select only environmentally friendly products. Some of these are quite esoteric and found only in outlets such as wholefood shops; others are available on ordinary supermarket shelves. More information about the chemical ingredients of household products can be found on the Friends of the Earth and Greenpeace websites (see 'Environmental organisations' in Addresses section for both of these). For further reading about the health risks associated with chemicals in cleaning products, see *Cleaning Yourself to Death: How safe is your home?* by Pat Thomas.

Consider buying products which are free of artificial fragrances and avoiding products such as air fresheners and scented carpet sprays. Try using a damp cloth instead of cleaning sprays, and if you want to improve the smell of your home, burn essential oils such as lavender in tea-light heated diffusers (for safety reasons, never leave these unattended). Be aware of the harmful effects of VOCs – if you are using strong cleaning products, paint or other DIY substances, make sure the room is as well-ventilated as possible. Remember to air your dry-cleaning thoroughly before you hang it up, as this is treated with VOCs. One suggested antidote to 'VOC syndrome' is to have a lot of houseplants around the home: these help to sanitise the air and create a healthier environment.

## Product labelling

The information displayed on product labels can tell you something about their contents, in particular whether they are very toxic or hazardous.

**Hazard symbols** are the highly visible orange-and-black warning squares; these tell you about the main dangers associated with the product. They should be read in conjunction with the risk phrases (see overleaf).

 'Harmful' or 'irritant'. This refers to substances which do not pose a serious health risk if inhaled or consumed. However, if you get the product on your skin it could still cause some problems.

 'Toxic' or 'very toxic'. This warns that a product may be very dangerous to spill on your skin, and that it will cause a serious health risk if you swallow it.

 'Corrosive'. These substances destroy living tissue, and are therefore highly dangerous if spilled or swallowed.

 'Flammable' or 'extremely flammable'. Great care must be taken not to bring these substances anywhere near a naked flame or electrical element. Many aerosols carry this warning sign.

**Tactile danger warnings** are raised triangle-shapes, and warn people who are unable to see the orange-and-black hazard warnings. They must appear on all products that carry any of the hazard symbols listed above.

**Risk phrases** are standard phrases which warn about the hazards associated with using a product. For example: 'risk of serious damage to eyes'.

**Safety phrases** are standard phrases which tell you about the precautions you need to take when using or storing a product. For example: 'use only in well ventilated areas'.

As we have noted, manufacturers are not required to list the **ingredients** of their products. However, an EC recommendation cites certain ingredients that should be labelled if they are present above a concentration of 0.2 per cent, and others (enzymes, preservatives, optical brighteners) that should be labelled regardless of concentration. Laundry detergents should carry detailed dosing instructions. Research shows that most products do carry the recommended information.

# Safety and first aid

Many cleaning chemicals are potentially hazardous, and accidents can easily happen in the course of cleaning jobs – particularly those involving ladders, hot substances or electrical appliances. Prevention is, of course, better than cure, so it is important to always observe the safety precautions detailed below. In the event of an accident, first-aid procedures are outlined here. If an injury is serious, call for medical help immediately, and do not attempt to administer more than basic treatment unless you are sure you know what you are doing.

## Safety precautions

- Prevent exposed areas of skin from coming into contact with chemicals★. Wear heavy-duty household gloves (thin disposable gloves may be weakened by strong chemicals).
- Make sure that no chemical, grit or sharp object gets into your eyes. Ordinary glasses provide some protection but safety goggles (from DIY shops) cover the whole area surrounding the eyes and are vital if you are doing a job such as scraping rust from metal windows. If you do get any chemical on your skin or in your eyes, rinse thoroughly with cold water. If stinging or burning persists, seek medical help.
- Avoid breathing in unpleasant, possibly toxic★, fumes. A face mask (from DIY shops) will help with this but you would be wise to keep the room well-ventilated, opening as many doors and windows as you can.
- Never use any flammable★ product in an area where there is a

★See Appendix I, Chemicals in cleaning products, for an explanation of the hazard symbols on cleaning product labels.

naked flame or electrical element – for example, an open or electric fire, a pilot light or an unextinguished cigarette.

- Make sure electrical appliances are in good working order. Do not touch them, or electrical sockets, with wet hands. Use the correct fuse for the appliance.
- Do not take unnecessary risks. For example, never do work that involves standing on a ladder if you are alone. If you fall and injure yourself you could find it difficult to get help.
- Do not leave cleaning equipment lying around, but clear up as you go along.
- Eliminate hazards as far as possible. Secure loose rugs with non-slip underlays, mop up spills as they occur and do not over-polish floors as this could make them slippery.
- Keep all cleaning products locked away if you have children, pets or elderly people in the household.

## Basic first-aid kit

Keep a basic first-aid kit in a well-marked container with a white cross on a green background in an accessible place (although out of reach to young hands) and replace any items that get used. You can buy ready-stocked kits, but you can cut the cost of these and have a more comprehensive version by making one up for yourself. Inspect the kit every year and check the contents, particularly medicines, to see that they have not gone beyond their use-by date. A basic household first-aid kit should include the following items:

- cotton bandages/contour bandages – one 5cm, one 7.5cm wide
- crêpe bandages – one 5cm, one 7.5cm wide
- triangular bandage
- Micropore tape
- plasters – 15 to 20 individually wrapped, some waterproof
- wound dressings, both medium and large sizes
- eye pad (an extra non-adhesive wound dressing can be used instead, but it needs to be large enough to cover the whole eye area)
- eye bath
- gauze swabs – at least four
- antiseptic wipes
- calamine lotion

- tweezers for getting out splinters
- safety pins
- strong scissors (strong enough to cut through fabric).

Stick the phone numbers of your GP's and dentist's surgeries, your pharmacist and the accident and emergency department of your nearest hospital on the inside of the lid. Keep a manual of first-aid procedures with the box too. If you are out at work and someone else is in your home – a childminder or a cleaner, say – leave your telephone number somewhere prominent.

## First-aid procedures

A lot of first-aid is plain common sense, but often that can go out of the window when dealing with someone who has suddenly been injured. Basic advice for treating injuries is given below. If the injury is not minor, either take the person to the accident and emergency department of your nearest hospital – if he or she can be moved – or dial 999 for an ambulance.

Be alert for signs of shock: these include clammy skin, rapid shallow breathing, dizziness, extreme thirst, weak pulse or fainting. If the person is in shock, lie him or her down, protecting the damaged area from contact with the ground, and (unless a leg fracture is suspected) raise and support the legs. Turn the person's head to one side to prevent choking, loosen any tight clothing, keep him or her warm and give sips of water. Call for emergency help.

The information given here is no substitute for first-aid training. Courses are available at your local British Red Cross branch.

### Cuts and wounds

A small blood loss can often look more than it actually is. Usually the bleeding stops of its own accord but occasionally it may not.

Seek medical help if:

- bleeding is severe *or* does not stop after 20 minutes
- shock develops (see above)
- the wound is a puncture injury, e.g. from a nail
- the cut is dirty, jagged or gaping.

## For a small wound or graze
- If possible, first wash your hands and wear disposable gloves if these are easily available.
- *Do not* attempt to dislodge any deeply embedded object.
- Remove any *loose* dirt or gravel, etc.
- Rinse under cold water.
- Gently clean the surrounding area, using a damp clean cloth or an antiseptic wipe, wiping *away* from the wound.
- If dirt or grit remains in a graze, use a clean soft nail brush or a toothbrush, ideally under cold running water.
- Pat the area dry with a clean, non-fluffy cloth.
- Cover a small wound with a plaster; for larger cuts or grazes use a sterile gauze pad and a bandage or plaster.

If blood continues to flow, apply pressure directly over the injured area, unless an object is embedded in it.

## For a larger wound
- Lie the person down, with the injured area raised.
- Press a clean cloth firmly over the wound, so that the wound edges are held together.
- Maintain this pressure continuously by bandaging a pad tightly over the cloth.
- If blood soaks through the pad, bandage another one over the top. *Do not* remove the original bandage and pad.

## If an object is embedded in the skin
- Loosely drape a clean cloth over the wound and the object.
- Build up pads of gauze around the wound until they are above the height of the object.
- Secure the pads with a firmly applied bandage, without bandaging over the object itself.
- Seek medical help.

## Splinters
Clean round the area with warm water and soap. Pass the ends of a pair of tweezers (not a needle) through a match flame, and allow them to cool. Without wiping the sterilised tweezers, try to pull out the splinter at the same angle that it went into the skin, grabbing it

as close as possible to the skin. When the splinter has come out squeeze the wound to make it bleed a little.

Take the person to the doctor if the splinter or part of it remains in the skin.

## Bruising

A bruise is caused by the seeping out of blood from injured blood vessels. In itself, bruising represents an injury to the soft tissues such as muscles or ligaments, but remember that it can also be a sign of a more serious injury such as a fracture (see below).

To reduce bruising and painful swelling to an injured part when no fracture is suspected, cool it for about 10–20 minutes – a bag of frozen peas with a damp tea-towel acting as a bandage round both the peas and the injury is ideal (*do not* put the ice in direct contact with the skin). This works by reducing the flow of blood to the injury. Make sure that the compression is not too tight, remembering to allow for a degree of swelling when applying the bandage. First-aid measures will not completely abolish the swelling.

## Sprains and strains

A sprain is a slight or partial tear in a ligament, often found near a joint, while a strain is a muscle injury. Like bruising, these are soft tissue injuries.

A good mnemonic for dealing with sprains is 'RICE':

- **R**est the injured part.
- Apply **I**ce or a cold compress (e.g. frozen peas wrapped in a tea-towel – see above) for 20 minutes every three to four hours.
- **C**ompress the injury with an elasticated stocking. The bandage should extend well above and below the injury and should not be so tight as to cut off the circulation. You can continue to apply ice (above) through the bandage.
- **E**levate the injured part so that it is above the heart, if possible.

## Broken bones

Sometimes it is obvious if there is a fracture, but sprains and strains can be just as painful as a fracture and can cause as much tenderness and swelling. If you suspect a fracture, the person will need to be taken to hospital for an X-ray.

- Try not to move a suspected broken arm or leg until it has been checked by a doctor. Support and secure the injured part so that it cannot move: put the arm into a sling; support other fractures with your hands and padding such as pillows, blankets, etc.
- In case a general anaesthetic is needed, do not give food or drink (except sips of water) to the person.
- Only move the person if it is really necessary. If you suspect an injury to the back or neck, do not move him or her at all – wait for emergency help.

### Burns and scalds

It is important to administer immediate relief for burns. However, if the burn is very deep, over a large area or is near the mouth and throat, the person should then be taken to hospital.

- Carefully remove any clothing that has been immersed in hot fat, boiling water or caustic chemicals, unless it has already stuck to the skin. Don't take off cooled, dry burnt clothes, as this could introduce infection.
- Flood the burnt or scalded area gently with cold water for at least ten minutes. If water is not available, use another cold liquid such as beer, milk or wine.
- Carefully remove jewellery and any constricting clothing before the injured area swells.
- Once cooled, the burn should be protected by a layer of clean covering which has no hairs or filaments, such as cotton, cling-film or a plastic bag.

---

**How to put out burning clothing**
- Stop the person panicking or running around.
- Lie him or her on the ground.
- If water is available, use it to put out the flames.
- If no water is available, wrap the person tightly in a blanket, coat or any other non-flammable material, and roll him or her over until the flames have been smothered.

---

**Do not:**
- Use an adhesive dressing, plaster or any fluffy material such as cotton wool.

- Apply any butter, grease, oil, lotion etc.
- Burst any blisters or remove loose skin, as this will increase the risk of introducing infection.

### Electric shock

Impress on children the importance of never playing with sockets, wires or flex, and of never bringing water into contact with an electrical appliance.

If someone has been in an electrical accident he or she needs to be removed from the source of electricity; however, you must be very careful not to touch him or her or you could get electrocuted yourself.

- Switch off the current at the mains. If you cannot do this, stand on dry material, such as wood or a book, and use a broom handle or chair leg to push the person away from the source of the electricity.
- *Do not* touch the person, but pull him or her right away by wrapping a dry cloth or towel round his or her legs.
- Call for emergency help.

### Poisoning

Keep all medicines, cleaning fluids, plant foods and so on out of reach and out of sight of children, in childproof cupboards. Review your storage arrangements as the child gets older and smarter, and take any medicines that are out of date or redundant to the pharmacist for disposal. Never decant poisonous substances into bottles previously used for drink, for instance, or that look in any way appealing.

See Chapter 9, Products that work, for an explanation of the hazard symbols on cleaning products, which indicate how serious a health risk they pose if inhaled or consumed.

If a poisonous substance is swallowed:

- *Do not* induce vomiting.
- Give the person frequent sips of water if he or she has swallowed a corrosive liquid, such as bleach.
- If the person is unconscious, check that the airway is clear of vomit and tilt the head back.
- Seek emergency help, taking any loose pills or suspect bottles with you; don't rely on your memory for names of medication that may have been swallowed.

- If a poisonous substance is inhaled, take the person into fresh air. Seek medical help.

### Head injury
If the person is unconscious, call for emergency help immediately.

- If any fluid is coming from the ear or nose, place a sterile dressing over the orifice and turn the person on to his or her injured side, but do not apply pressure or try to block the flow.
- If there is a cut on the scalp or face, the bleeding will be profuse. Try to stop the bleeding by applying constant pressure with a sterile dressing or clean cloth, but if there is a foreign body or fragment of bone in the wound, cover the area without pressing on it.
- If there is a bump on the head, apply an ice pack (or a bag of frozen peas wrapped in a cold, wet tea towel) to reduce the pain and swelling.
- Keep a close watch on the person until medical help arrives.

# Addresses

When looking for a specialist cleaner it is advisable to choose a member of a trade organisation, if appropriate, since they are usually helpful and prepared to arbitrate in the case of complaints. Many trade organisations operate a code of practice agreed with the Office of Fair Trading. The symbol † below denotes a trade organisation that operate such a code of practice.

## Antiques

**British Antique Dealers' Association**
20 Rutland Gate
London SW7 1BD
Tel: 020-7589 4128
Fax: 020-7581 9083
Email: enquiry@bada.demon.co.uk
Website: www.bada.org
*Information on caring for antique carpets and rugs, clocks, furniture, prints, silver, watercolours and paintings*

**†LAPADA – The Association of Art and Antique Dealers**
535 Kings Road
London SW10 0SZ
Tel: 020-7823 3511
Fax: 020-7823 3522
Email: lapada@lapada.co.uk
Website: www.lapada.co.uk

## Auctioneers

*To check whether articles in your possession are valuable*

**Christie's International Ltd**
85 Old Brompton Road
London SW7 3LD
Tel: 020-7581 7611
Fax: 020-7321 3321
Website: www.christies.com

**Bonhams**
101 New Bond Street
London W1S 1SR
Tel: 020-7629 6602
Fax: 020-7629 8876
Website: www.bonhams.com

**Sothebys**
34–35 New Bond Street
London W1A 2AA
Tel: 020-7293 5000
Fax: 020-7293 5989
Website: www.sothebys.com

## Asthma

**The British Allergy Foundation**
Deepdene House
30 Bellegrove Road
Welling, Kent DA16 3PY
Tel: 020-8303 8583 (*helpline*)
Fax: 020-8303 8792
Email: info@allergyfoundation.com
Website:
www.allergyfoundation.com

**National Asthma Campaign**
Providence House
Providence Place
London N1 0NT
Tel: (08457) 010203 (*helpline, open Mon–Fri 9–7*)
020-7226 2260 (*office*)
Fax: 020-7704 0740
Website: www.asthma.org.uk

## Blinds

**The British Blind and Shutter Association**
42 Heath Street
Tamworth, Staffs B79 7JH
Tel: (01827) 52337
Fax: (01827) 310827
Website: www.bbsa.co.uk
*Will provide contact details of members who can clean all types of blind*

## Books

**Antiquarian Booksellers' Association**
Sackville House
40 Piccadilly
London W1J 0DR
Tel: 020-7439 3118
Fax: 020-7439 3119
Email: info@aba.org.uk
Website:
www.ABAinternational.com
*Any ABA member can advise on the cleaning and conservation of antiquarian books. List of members available free on application, and also available on the website.*

## Building materials

**British Cement Association**
Century House
Telford Avenue
Crowthorne
Berkshire RG45 6YS
Tel: (01344) 762676
Fax: (01344) 761214
Website: www.bca.org.uk

**The Building Centre**
26 Store Street
London WC1E 7BT
Tel: 020-7692 4000 (*office*)
(09065) 161136 (*advice on products, materials and trade names*)
(09065) 161137 (*technical advice*)
Fax: 020-7580 9641
Email: manu@buildingcentre.co.uk
Website: www.buildingcentre.co.uk

## Carpets

†**The Carpet Council**
See *The Carpet Foundation*

**The Carpet Foundation**
MCF Complex
60 New Road
Kidderminster
Worcestershire DY10 1AQ
Tel: (01562) 755568
Fax: (01562) 865405
Website:
www.carpetfoundation.com

**British Carpet Technical Centre**
Wira House
West Park Ring Road
Leeds LS16 6QL
Tel: 0113-259 1999
Fax: 0113-278 0306
Email: bctc@wira.u-net.com
Website: www.bttg.co.uk
*Advice on technical problems with carpets*

**National Carpet Cleaners Association Ltd**
62C London Road
Oadby
Leicester LE2 5DH
Tel: 0116-271 9550
Fax: 0116-271 9588
Website: www.ncca.co.uk
*Members required to maintain specified standards for cleaning carpets and upholstery and operate an extensive code of practice. The Association's specialist Fire and Flood Division has expertise in dealing with fire and flood damage.*

**Thames Carpet Cleaners**
48–56 Reading Road
Henley-on-Thames
Oxon RG9 1AG
Tel: (01491) 574676
Fax: (01491) 577877
*Offer a rug-cleaning service and provide advice on carpet-cleaning products*

## Cars

†*Society of Motor Manufacturers and Traders Ltd*
Forbes House, Halkin Street
London SW1X 7DS
Tel: 020-7235 7000
Fax: 020-7235 7112
Website: www.smmt.co.uk

## Ceramics

**Bathroom Manufacturers' Association**
Federation House
Station Road
Stoke on Trent
Staffs ST4 2RT
Tel: (01782) 747123
Fax: (01782) 747161
Email:
info@bathroom-association.org.uk
Website:
www.bathroom-association.org

## Chimney cleaning

**National Association of Chimney Sweeps**
Unit 15
Emerald Way
Stone Business Park
Stone
Staffs ST15 0SR
Tel: (01785) 811732
(0800) 833464 *(freephone)*
Fax: (01785) 811712
*Will provide contact details of registered chimney sweeps*

## Cleaning cloths

**Vale Mill (Rochdale) Ltd**
Robinson Street
Rochdale LL16 1TA
Tel: (01706) 353535
Fax: (01706) 716128
*Supplier of a wide range of Minky cloths for cleaning specific materials*

## Cleaning for people with disabilities

**Age Concern England**
Astral House
1268 London Road
London SW16 4ER
Tel: 020-8765 7200
Fax: 020-8765 7211
Email: ace@ace.org.uk
Website: www.ace.org.uk

**Age Concern Northern Ireland**
3 Lower Crescent
Belfast BT7 1NR
Tel: 028-9024 5729
Fax: 028-9023 5497
Email: info@ageconcernni.org

**Age Concern Scotland**
113 Rose Street
Edinburgh EH2 3DT
Tel: 0131-220 3345
Fax: 0131-220 2779
Email: acs@ccis.org.uk

*Age Concern Cymru*
4th Floor, 1 Cathedral Road
Cardiff CF11 9SD
Tel: 029-2037 1566
Fax: 029-2039 9562
Email: enquiries@accymru.org.uk
Website: www.accymru.org.uk

*Advice on help to which those with
disabilities may be entitled is available
from any of the above*

**Chestercare**
PO Box 5665
Kirkby-in-Ashfield
Notts NG17 7QX
Tel: (01623) 757955/720005
Fax: (01623) 755585
Email: sales@snrehab.com
*Mail-order catalogue featuring useful
cleaning aids*

**Disabled Living Foundation**
380–384 Harrow Road
London W9 2HU
Tel: 020-7289 6111 *(office)*
(0845) 130 9177 *(helpline)*
Fax: 020-7266 2922
Textphone: 020-7432 8009
Email: dlfinfo@dlf.org.uk
Website: www.dlf.org.uk
*Permanent display of equipment, some of
which helps with cleaning, may be seen
at this address and at centres around
Britain*

**Keep Able Store**
38C Telford Way
Kettering
Northants NN16 8UN
Tel: (01536) 525153
Fax: (01536) 515077
*Mail-order catalogue*

## Conservation

*See also 'Books', 'Paintings and pictures'
and 'Textiles'*

**UK Institute for Conservation of
Historic and Artistic Works**
109 The Chandlery
50 Westminster Bridge Road
London SE1 7QY
Tel: 020-7721 8721
Fax: 020-7721 8722
Email: ukic@ukic.org.uk
Website: www.ukic.org.uk
*The Institute holds a register of
conservators and for a small fee will
supply names and addresses*

## Cork

**The Cork Industry Federation**
13 Felton Lea
Sidcup
Kent DA14 6BA
Tel/Fax: 020-8302 4801
Website: www.cork-products.co.uk
*Advice on care of cork finishes*

## Craftsmen

**The Guild of Master Craftsmen**
166 High Street
Lewes
East Sussex BN7 1XU
Tel: (01273) 478449
Fax: (01273) 478606
*Register of members who are able to clean
damaged craft items*

## Dry-cleaners

**Brooks Services Group**
210 Aztec West
Almondsbury
Bristol BS32 4SN
Tel: (01454) 614668
Fax: (01454) 201075
Email:
info@brooks-service-group.co.uk
Website:
www.brooks-service-group.co.uk

**Elias Hand Finished Dry Cleaners**
68 St John's Wood High Street
London NW8 7SH
Tel: 020-7586 3424
Fax: 020-7483 0270

**Harry Berger**
25 Station Road
Cheadle Hulme
Cheshire SK8 5AF
Tel: 0161-485 3421
Fax: 0161-282 2860
Email: harryberger@emailx.co.uk
*In addition to dry cleaning, offer domestic dyeing*

**Johnson Service Group Cleaners**
Mildmay Road
Bootle
Merseyside L20 5EW
Tel: 0151-933 6161
Fax: 0151-922 8089

**Lewis & Wayne Ltd**
9 Streatham High Road
London SW16 1DZ
Tel: 020-8769 8777
Fax: 020-8769 8779
Website:
www.lewiswayne.fsnet.co.uk

**Sunlight Service Group Ltd**
111 Parkview
Whitley Bay
Tyne and Wear NE26 3RH
Tel: 0191-251 0770
Fax: 0191-251 0737

*All the above dry-cleaning companies have a number of branches capable of high-quality dry-cleaning of items such as designer evening wear, wedding dresses, antique christening robes and other valuable textiles or those which are of sentimental value*

**Dry Cleaning Information Bureau**
7 Churchill Court
58 Station Road
North Harrow
Middlesex HA2 7SA
Tel: 020-8863 8658
Fax: 020-8861 2115
Email: tsa-uk.org
Website: www.tsa-uk.org

**Textile Services Association**
*See below under 'Textiles'*

# Electrical appliances

†*The Association of Manufacturers of Domestic Electrical Appliances (AMDEA)*
Rapier House
40–46 Lambs Conduit Street
London WC1N 3NW
Tel: 020-7405 0666
Fax: 020-7405 6609
Email: info@amdea.org.uk

# Enamelled products

**Vitreous Enamel Association**
16 Cameron Court
Winwick Quay
Warrington
WA2 8RE
Tel: (07071) 226716
Fax: (01925) 417827

# Environmental organisations

**Friends of the Earth**
26–28 Underwood Street
London N1 7JQ
Tel: 020-7490 1555
Fax: 020-7490 0881
Email: info@foe.co.uk
Website: www.foe.co.uk

**Greenpeace**
Canonbury Villas
London N1 2PN
Tel: 020-7865 8100
Fax: 020-7865 8200
Email: info@uk.greenpeace.org
Website: www.greenpeace.org.uk

## Floor polish

**S.C. Johnson**
Frimley Green
Camberley
Surrey GU16 7AJ
Tel: (01276) 852000 (*office*)
(0800) 353353 (*Homecare line*)
Fax: (01179) 156693
Email:
scj-homecareline@ukcentral.com
Website: www.scjohnson.com

## Footwear

**British Footwear Association**
3 Burystead Place
Wellingborough
Northants NN8 1AH
Tel: (01933) 229005
Fax: (01933) 225009
Email: bfa@easynet.co.uk
Website: www.britfoot.com

**SATRA Footwear Technology Centre**
SATRA House
Rockingham Road
Kettering
Northants NN16 9JH
Tel: (01536) 410000
Fax: (01536) 410626
Email: admin@satra.co.uk
Website: www.satra.co.uk

## Fungicidal treatment

**Dax Products Ltd**
PO Box 119
Nottingham NG3 5NA
Tel: 0115-926 9996
Fax: 0115-966 1173
Website: www.daxproducts.co.uk
*Supplier of Fungo*

## Furniture

*See also 'Upholstery'*

**British Furniture Manufacturers Ltd**
30 Harcourt Street
London W1H 2AA
Tel: 020-7724 0851
Fax: 020-7706 1924
Email: enquiries@bfm.org.uk
Website: www.bfm.org.uk

## Furniture polish

**Picreator Enterprises**
44 Park View Gardens
Hendon
London NW4 2PN
Tel: 020-8202 8972
Fax: 020-8202 3435
*Supplier by mail of Renaissance wax furniture polish*

## General cleaning products

**Kleeneze Europe Ltd**
Martins Road
Hanham
Bristol BS15 3DY
Tel: 0117-967 0861
Fax: 0117-975 0312
Email:
servicecentre@kleeneze.co.uk
Website: www.kleeneze.co.uk
*Door-to-door suppliers of a wide range of cleaning products. Ask for an agent to call*

## Glass

**Glass and Glazing Federation**
44–48 Borough High Street
London SE1 1XB
Tel: 020-7403 7177
Fax: 020-7357 7458
Email: info@ggf.org.uk
Website: www.ggf.org.uk
*Information on cleaning all types of glass*

**Ritec International Ltd**
15 Royal London Estate
West Road
London N17 0XL
Tel: 020-8885 5155
Fax: 020-8885 5072
Email: admin@ritec.co.uk
Website: www.ritec.co.uk
*Supplier of Clear-shield solution*

## Hand deodoriser

**Divertimenti Ltd**
44 Fulham Road
London SW3 6HH
Tel: 020-7823 8151
Fax: 020-7581 2764
Website: www.divertimenti.co.uk
*Supplier by mail of Fresh Hands product*

## Insurance

**The Association of British Insurers**
51 Gresham Street
London EC2V 7HQ
Tel: 020-7600 3333
Fax: 020-7696 8999
Email: info@abi.org.uk
Website: www.abi.org.uk

## Laundry

*See also 'Textiles'*

**British Apparel and Textile Confederation (BATC)**
5 Portland Place
London W1B 1PW
Tel: 020-7636 7788
Fax: 020-7636 7515
Email: batc@dial.pipex.com
Website: www.batc.co.uk
*Advice on washcare symbols and dry-cleaning mishaps*

**Dylon International Ltd**
Worsley Lower Sydenham
Bridge Road
London SE26 5HD
Tel: 020-8663 4296
Email: DylonInt@dylon.co.uk
Website: www.dylon.co.uk
*Consumer advice bureau on laundry aid products, fabric dyes and stain removers*

**Home Laundering Consultative Council**
5 Portland Place
London W1B 1PW
Tel: 020-7636 7788
Fax: 020-7636 7515
Website: www.care-labelling.com

**Lever Fabergé Ltd**
Lever House
3 St James's Road
Kingston-upon-Thames
Surrey KT1 2BA
Tel: 020-8439 6000
Website: www.leveruk.com
*Advice on washing and products*

**Procter & Gamble Ltd**
Cobalt 12
Silver Fox Way
Cobalt Business Park
Newcastle upon Tyne NE27 0QW
Tel: 0191-297 8218
Fax: 0191-297 5096
Website: www.pg.com
*Advice on washing and products*

## Leather

**Connolly Leather Ltd**
The Boulevard
Orbital Park
Ashford
Kent TN24 0SA
Tel: (01233) 501100
Fax: (01233) 501199
*Advice on caring for leather (ask for Renovation department)*

## Mildew

**Picreator Enterprises**
(see above under 'Furniture polish')
*Supplier by mail of Mystox mildew
treatment*

## Motorcycles

**Motor Cycle Industry Association Ltd**
Starley House
Eaton Road
Coventry CV1 2FH
Tel: (08700) 706242
Fax: (08700) 703291
Website: www.mcia.co.uk

## Office equipment

**Fellowes Ltd**
Yorkshire Way
West Moor Park
Doncaster
DN3 3FB
Tel: (01302) 885331
Fax: (01302) 890003
Website: www.fellowes.com
*Office equipment cleaning supplies*

## Outdoor clothing

**Nikwax**
Durgates Industrial Estate
Wadhurst
East Sussex TN5 6DF
Tel: (01892) 783855
Fax: (01892) 783748
Website: www.nikwax.co.uk
*Reproofing of outdoor wear, such as
Gore-Tex*

## Paintings and pictures

**Association of British Picture
Restorers**
Station Avenue
Kew, Surrey TW9 3QA
Tel/Fax: 020-8948 5644
Email: abprlondon@aol.com
Website: www.abpr.co.uk
*Restoration advice*

## Pest control

**British Pest Control Association**
1 Gleneagles House
Vernon Gate
South Street
Derby DE1 1UP
Tel: (01332) 294288
Fax: (01332) 295904
Email: enquiry@BPCA.org.uk
Website: www.BPCA.org.uk
*List of recommended specialist pest control
contractors*

**Rentokil Initial plc**
Felcourt
East Grinstead
West Sussex RH19 2JY
Tel: (01342) 833022
Fax: (01342) 326229
Website:
www.rentokil-initial.com

**Terminix**
Heritage House
234 High Street
Sutton
Surrey SM1 1NX
Tel: 020-8661 6600
Fax: 020-8642 0677
Website: www.terminix.co.uk
*Advice on pest control. Supplier of fly
screens and bird mesh*

## Pianos

**Heckscher & Co**
75 Bayham Street
London NW1 0AA
Tel: 020-7387 1735
Fax: 020-7387 3043
Email: sales@heckscher.co.uk
Website:
www.uk-piano.org/heckscher
*Suppliers of a range of cleaning products
for pianos including key polishes, polishes
for polyester-finished cases and for
French-polished cases*

## Plastics

**British Plastics Federation**
6 Bath Place
Rivington Street
London EC2A 3JE
Tel: 020-7457 5000
Fax: 020-7457 5045
Email: bpf@bpf.co.uk
Website: www.bpf.co.uk

## Range cookers

**Aga-Rayburn**
Station Road
Ketley, Telford
Shropshire TF1 5AQ
Tel: (01952) 642000
Fax: (01952) 222048
Email: info@aga-rayburn.co.uk
Website: www.aga-rayburn.co.uk
*Advice on cleaning range cookers*

## Silver storage

**The Tarnprufe Co**
68 Nether Edge Road
Sheffield S7 1RX
Tel: 0114-255 3652
Fax: 0114-250 9887
*Supplier of bags and cutlery rolls for storing silver and silver-cleaning mitts*

## Stain removers

**The Beckmann Stain Advisory Service**
ACDOCO
Imperial Works
Mallison Street
Bolton
Lancashire BL1 8PP
Tel: (01204) 600500
Fax: (01204) 600501
Email: specialist@acdo.co.uk
Website: www.acdo.co.uk
*Supplier of Stain Devil products for specific stains*

**Mykal Industries**
Farnsworth House
5 Morris Close
Park Farm Industrial Estate
Wellingborough
Northants NN8 6XF
Tel: (01933) 402822
Fax: (01933) 402488
Email: mykalind@aol.com
Website: www.mykal.co.uk
*Supplier of Manger's De-Solv-It*

## Textiles

*See also 'Dry-cleaners', 'Laundry' and 'Upholstery'*

**British Textile Technology Group (BTTG)**
Wira House
West Park Ring Road
Leeds LS16 6QL
Tel: 0113-259 1999
Fax: 0113-278 0306
Website: www.bttg.co.uk

**Lakeland Limited**
Alexandra Buildings
Windermere
Cumbria LA23 1BQ
Tel: (01539) 488100
Fax: (01539) 488300
Website: www.lakelandlimited.co.uk
*Supplier of net bags for delicate items which need machine-washing and net racks for drying items flat, plus a comprehensive range of cleaning products by mail order*

**Royal School of Needlework**
Apartment 12A
Hampton Court Palace
Surrey KT8 9AU
Tel: 020-8943 1432
Fax: 020-8943 4910
Email: rnwork@intonet.co.uk
Website:
www.royal-needlework.co.uk
*Cleaning and repair of embroidery and needlework*

**The Textile Conservation Centre**
University of Southampton
Winchester Campus
Park Avenue
Winchester SO23 8DL
Tel: 023-8059 7100
Fax: 023-8059 7101
Email: tccuk@soton.ac.uk
Website: www.soton.ac.uk-
wsart/tcc.htm
*Advice on the conservation of valuable
textiles*

**The Textile Conservation Studio**
Blickling Hall
Blickling
Aylsham
Norwich NR11 6NF
Tel: (01263) 733471
Fax: (01263) 734924

**The Textile Restoration Studio**
2 Talbot Road
Bowdon
Cheshire WA14 3JD
Tel/Fax: 0161-928 0020
Email:
studio@textilerestoration.co.uk
Website:
www.textilerestoration.co.uk
www.conservationconsortium.com
*Specialists in the cleaning and repair of
antique textiles. Product catalogue
available*

**Textile Services Association Ltd**
7 Churchill Court
58 Station Road
North Harrow
Middlesex HA2 7SA
Tel: 020-8863 7755
Fax: 020-8861 2115
Email: tsa@uk.org
Website: www.tsa-uk.org
*Telephone for details of specialist dry-
cleaners and laundries*

# Upholstery

*See also National Carpet Cleaners
Association, under 'Carpets'*

**British Interior Textile Association**
5 Portland Place
London W1B 1PW
Tel: 020-7636 7788
Fax: 020-7636 7515
Email: batc@dial.pipex.com

# Watchdogs

**Advertising Standards Authority
(ASA)**
2 Torrington Place
London WC1E 7HW
Tel: 020-7580 5555
Fax: 020-7631 3051
Email: inquiries@asa.org.uk
Website: www.asa.org.uk
*Complaints about non-broadcast
advertisements must be submitted in
writing*

**Consumers' Association**
2 Marylebone Road
London NW1 4DF
Tel: 020-7770 7000
Fax: 020-7770 7600
Email: which@which.net
Website: www.which.net

# Wigs

**Raoul Wigmakers**
34 Craven Road
Paddington
London W2 3QA
Tel: 020-7723 6914
Fax: 020-7402 5800
*Wig cleaner and supplier*

# Index

## WHICH? BOOKS

The following titles were available as this book went to press.

*General reference (legal, financial, practical, etc.)*

| | | |
|---|---|---|
| Be Your Own Financial Adviser | 432pp | £9.99 |
| 420 Legal Problems Solved | 352pp | £9.99 |
| 150 Letters that Get Results | 336pp | £9.99 |
| What to Do When Someone Dies | 176pp | £9.99 |
| The Which? Computer Troubleshooter | 192pp | £12.99 |
| The Which? Guide to an Active Retirement | 530pp | £12.99 |
| The Which? Guide to Changing Careers | 352pp | £10.99 |
| The Which? Guide to Choosing a Career | 336pp | £9.99 |
| The Which? Guide to Choosing a School | 336pp | £10.99 |
| The Which? Guide to Computers | 352pp | £10.99 |
| The Which? Guide to Computers for Small Businesses | 352pp | £10.99 |
| The Which? Guide to Divorce | 368pp | £10.99 |
| The Which? Guide to Doing Your Own Conveyancing | 208pp | £9.99 |
| The Which? Guide to Domestic Help | 208pp | £9.99 |
| The Which? Guide to Employment | 304pp | £10.99 |
| The Which? Guide to Gambling | 288pp | £9.99 |
| The Which? Guide to Getting Married | 224pp | £9.99 |
| The Which? Guide to Giving and Inheriting | 256pp | £9.99 |
| The Which? Guide to Going Digital | 272pp | £10.99 |
| The Which? Guide to Home Safety and Security | 198pp | £9.99 |
| The Which? Guide to Insurance | 320pp | £10.99 |
| The Which? Guide to the Internet | 320pp | £10.99 |
| The Which? Guide to Money | 448pp | £9.99 |
| The Which? Guide to Money on the Internet | 256pp | £9.99 |
| The Which? Guide to Pensions | 336pp | £9.99 |
| The Which? Guide to Renting and Letting | 336pp | £10.99 |

| | | |
|---|---|---|
| The Which? Guide to Shares | 288pp | £9.99 |
| The Which? Guide to Shopping on the Internet | 272pp | £10.99 |
| The Which? Guide to Starting Your Own Business | 288pp | £10.99 |
| The Which? Guide to Working from Home | 256pp | £9.99 |
| Which? Way to Buy, Own and Sell a Flat | 288pp | £10.99 |
| Which? Way to Buy, Sell and Move House | 320pp | £10.99 |
| Which? Way to Clean It | 256pp | £9.99 |
| Which? Way to Drive Your Small Business | 240pp | £10.99 |
| Which? Way to Manage Your Time – and Your Life | 208pp | £9.99 |
| Which? Way to Save and Invest | 464pp | £14.99 |
| Which? Way to Save Tax | 320pp | £14.99 |
| Wills and Probate | 224pp | £10.99 |

| | | |
|---|---|---|
| Make Your Own Will | 28pp | £10.99 |

Action Pack (A5 wallet with forms and 28-page book inside)

## Health

| | | |
|---|---|---|
| Understanding HRT and the Menopause | 256pp | £9.99 |
| The Which? Guide to Children's Health | 288pp | £9.99 |
| The Which? Guide to Complementary Medicine | 270pp | £9.99 |
| The Which? Guide to Managing Asthma | 256pp | £9.99 |
| The Which? Guide to Managing Back Trouble | 160pp | £9.99 |
| The Which? Guide to Managing Stress | 252pp | £9.99 |
| The Which? Guide to Men's Health | 336pp | £9.99 |
| The Which? Guide to Personal Health | 320pp | £10.99 |
| The Which? Guide to Women's Health | 448pp | £9.99 |
| Which? Medicine | 544pp | £12.99 |

## Gardening

| | | |
|---|---|---|
| The Gardening Which? Guide to Growing Your Own Vegetables | 224pp | £18.99 |

| | | |
|---|---|---|
| The Gardening Which? Guide to Patio and Container Plants | 224pp | £17.99 |
| The Gardening Which? Guide to Small Gardens | 224pp | £12.99 |
| The Gardening Which? Guide to Successful Perennials | 224pp | £17.99 |
| The Gardening Which? Guide to Successful Propagation | 158pp | £12.99 |
| The Gardening Which? Guide to Successful Pruning | 240pp | £12.99 |
| The Gardening Which? Guide to Successful Shrubs | 224pp | £12.99 |

## Do-it-yourself

| | | |
|---|---|---|
| The Which? Book of Do-It-Yourself | 320pp | £14.99 |
| The Which? Book of Plumbing and Central Heating | 160pp | £13.99 |
| The Which? Book of Wiring and Lighting | 160pp | £16.99 |
| Which? Way to Fix It | 208pp | £12.99 |

## Travel/leisure

| | | |
|---|---|---|
| The Good Bed and Breakfast Guide | 640pp | £14.99 |
| The Good Food Guide | 736pp | £15.99 |
| The Good Skiing and Snowboarding Guide | 592pp | £15.99 |
| The Good Walks Guide | 320pp | £13.99 |
| The Which? Guide to Country Pubs | 576pp | £13.99 |
| The Which? Guide to Pub Walks | 256pp | £9.99 |
| The Which? Guide to Scotland | 528pp | £12.99 |
| The Which? Guide to Tourist Attractions | 544pp | £12.99 |
| The Which? Guide to Weekend Breaks in Britain | 528pp | £13.99 |
| The Which? Hotel Guide | 752pp | £15.99 |
| The Which? Wine Guide | 512pp | £14.99 |
| Which? Holiday Destination | 624pp | £12.99 |

Available from bookshops, and by post from:
Which?, Dept TAZM, Castlemead,
Gascoyne Way, Hertford X, SG14 1LH
*or* phone FREE on (0800) 252100
quoting Dept TAZM and your credit card details

# The Which? Guide to Shopping on the Internet

For over 40 years Consumers' Association, through its magazine *Which?*, has been the prime source of buying wisdom for consumers throughout Britain.

Now, as more and more of us are using the 'mouse to house' route for buying goods and services, this new *Which?* guide offers not just the best-available advice for ensuring hassle-free purchases, but an extensive A–Z directory of web sites, including those belonging to members of the Which? Web Trader accreditation scheme. Here you'll find sites selling everything from books and CDs to computer kit, electrical goods, holidays, houses and cars – plus many more items you'd never have known were out there.

And, of course, the guide explains how to avoid the downside of shopping on the Net, especially the companies that disappear with your money; what your rights are and your routes to redress if things go wrong. It shows you: what you need to go shopping online; where to look, including shopping directories, portal sites, virtual malls and discount stores; what to look for in a good, easy-to-use site; how to track down unusual items; and how to buy from abroad. It also explains how auctions work on the Net.

Save time, money and hassle, and shop with complete confidence, using *The Which? Guide to Shopping on the Internet*.

Paperback       210 x 120mm       272 pages       £10.99

Available from bookshops, and by post from
Which?, Dept TAZM, Castlemead,
Gascoyne Way, Hertford X, SG14 1LH
*or* phone FREE on (0800) 252100
quoting Dept TAZM and your credit card details

# The Good Skiing & Snowboarding Guide

'Telling it like it is means this thoroughly researched guide can save you from rogues and rip-offs as you head for the snow . . . Essential pre-piste reading.'
*Men's Health*

*The Good Skiing and Snowboarding Guide* is the only independent reference book for anyone planning a winter sports holiday. As it carries no advertising or sponsorship it is able to offer truly unbiased information to help you choose the right resort.

Award-winning ski journalists Peter and Felice Hardy present pithy and pertinent assessments of not just the ski resorts but the ski schools, the accommodation, the nightlife and the food in over 650 resorts on five continents.

This guide includes:
- key facts for each major resort, such as the transfer time from the nearest major airport, number of lifts, lift pass prices, concessions available, facilities for children and food and drink prices
- evaluation of each resort's suitability for snowboarders, children, beginners, intermediates and advanced skiers
- a look at other winter sports available in resorts
- coverage of North American resorts
- an extensive directory of travel contacts, including tour operators, skiing and snowboarding organisations

Paperback    210 x 120mm    592 pages    £15.99

Available from bookshops, and by post from
Which?, Dept TAZM, Castlemead,
Gascoyne Way, Hertford X, SG14 1LH
*or* phone FREE on (0800) 252100
quoting Dept TAZM and your credit card details

# The Gardening Which? Guide to Growing Your Own Vegetables

'I would recommend this book to any enthusiastic vegetable grower . . . enticing and easy to follow.'
*The Garden*

Nothing tastes as good as vegetables freshly gathered from the garden – but how can you ensure that the time and effort you put into growing them does not result in disappointment? *The Gardening Which? Guide to Growing Your Own Vegetables* has the answers.

This practical and inspiring guide shows you in words and pictures how to grow some 50 types of vegetables, with selected varieties based on *Gardening Which?* trials and taste tests. The range includes some of the more unusual salad items and exotics now available in supermarkets, and around two dozen herbs. Symbols on each vegetable entry indicate which are easy to grow or high-yielding and a calendar takes you step by step through the planting and harvesting of each vegetable. And you don't need a dedicated vegetable plot or an allotment – many of the vegetables can be grown in containers, borders or raised beds.

Pest control, routine soil care, fertilisers, watering, overwintering and the common problems affecting vegetables are covered throughout. Whether you want to be self-sufficient, or just save money on some of the pricier items available in the shops, this guide will help you get the most from your garden.

Hardback    252 x 193mm    224 pages    £18.99

Available from bookshops, and by post from:
Which?, Dept TAZM, Castlemead,
Gascoyne Way, Hertford X, SG14 1LH
*or* phone FREE on (0800) 252100
quoting Dept TAZM and your credit card details